NGLE

MURDO MACDONALD

# RUSKIN'S TRIANGLE

MA BIBLIOTHÈQUE

MURDO MACDONALD

# RUSKIN'S TRIANGLE

THE CONSTELLATIONS, BOOK XXI

MA BIBLIOTHÈQUE, LONDON

 Published 2021

Printed by Printed World Publishing, Hastings, Great Britain

Set in Didot and Bodoni Ornaments

ISBN 978-1-910055-87-8



Papers used are from well-managed forests and responsible sources



MA BIBLIOTHÈQUE

BEGUN 23 MARCH 2014
CONCLUDED 17 SEPTEMBER 2016
EDITED FOR PUBLICATION SPRING 2021

*Thanks are due to my first readers,*
*Andrew Randall and Ian Stephen*

人

IT IS SAID THAT RUSKIN could not tolerate the beauty of the triangle of hair that points to the loveliness of a woman's cunt. So, in a spirit of solidarity—for Ruskin, however much I may disagree with him, is a kindred spirit—I will write about his difficulty in sympathy with his uneasy sexuality, which can, perhaps, stand in for the uneasy sexuality of the West. Some say that Ruskin's understanding was not as distorted by ignorance as posterity would have it. That may be so but nevertheless his sexual life was not settled into what one might call a normal pattern. But then, whose is? Freud, as translated by Bruno Bettelheim, writes of 'the uneasiness inherent in culture'. Quite so.

But to begin I reflect on how Ruskin saved me in Venice. It was my first visit to that city. Perhaps I had not been before because I did not want to risk disappointment or perhaps because I believe that places come along at the right time and there is no point in hurrying a visit to somewhere of significance. That morning I was trying to find a library. Getting off the train I noticed some graffiti. Italian graffiti, like all graffiti, ranges from the well judged to the over enthusiastic. This particular example was somewhere in the middle. Earlier in the day I had been enjoying the graffiti in Padua. There was one artist in particular who had written the lines of a love song one by one around the city. Petrarch would have been intrigued. Coming out of the modernist railway terminus of Venezia Santa Lucia I was dazzled by the sunlight breaking off the Grand Canal. Venice is a city that lets you know when you have arrived. I wandered a bit, crossing canals by small bridges and finding myself in streets often no more than passageways between high, close buildings. I followed signs for San Marco but as I got closer to my destination the density of tourists increased until in a state of near complete alienation I entered the square and saw nothing but people. I had an impulse to go straight back to Padua, which – having lived there for all of a week – by then I regarded as home. But then Ruskin saved Venice for me for I began to see the detail of the place as he had. No one else seemed interested in that detail so I found myself alone, private and contemplative in that vast crowd, in the company of sunned panels of carefully chosen marble and intricately designed capitals carved with botanical motifs. When Ruskin looked at Venice he stepped forward to look and so did I. Every detail became for him not so much a detail in itself as a detail indicative of a city, a part that implied the whole. On the exterior of St Mark's as it begins to link to the Ducal Palace some of the marble panels are stabilised by metal pegs. Those pegs serve to emphasise the beauty of the stone as a slight limp may make a beautiful woman's movement even more perfect, or as the deliberate error in an oriental carpet dedicates it to God. And that imperfect perfection is made the more so by warmth, for the light of those panels warms the gaze like the light of a harvest moon as though the light were not merely reflected but created.

In due course, I found the library. It had been hiding in plain sight, for it occupied one complete side of the Piazzetta. Indeed, I found I had already photographed the hulking statues at its entrance. On entering, the Venice of tourism ceased as though it had never existed. At first I thought the reading room was presided over by a bust of Dante but later I realised that it was Petrarch, who had given his collection of books to found the place. Or rather that collection would have founded the library had it not been allowed to moulder away to nothing in a sad if typical misstep in the great and enduring failure of understanding between every municipality and its intellectual class. Such loss is always felt keenly however many centuries have passed. In this case, it was an accidental iconoclasm, an iconoclasm of omission. In others, like the burning of the library at Alexandria, such iconoclasm is notably deliberate. Thomas Browne says of the deliberate iconoclast: 'But the iniquity of oblivion blindly scattereth her poppy, and deals with the memory of men without distinction to merit of perpetuity. Who can but pity the founder of the pyramids? Herostratus lives that burnt the temple of Diana, he is almost lost that built it'. Not always true, but he has a point.

Ruskin is thought to be the most English of critics but an awareness of iconoclasm was part and parcel of his Scottish background. His family had close links with Perth, a city that through the excessive enthusiasm of the inhabitants for the preaching of the Geneva-educated John Knox, helped to drive the iconoclasm that was to be a feature of the Reformation in Scotland. Yet Ruskin's connection with Perth is most remembered for the failure of his marriage to his cousin Effie Gray. The myth or the reality is that Ruskin could not tolerate the difference between the smoothed over female genitals, or rather non-genitals, of the marble statues of the Greeks and Romans and the sexual presence of his wife. What is interesting is that this myth or truth was ever convincing.

It is curious, perhaps in itself iconoclastic, to think of the ancient Greeks as mutilators of female genitals in their visual art. What they did was not idealising. It was a question of removal. To idealise is to attempt to make formally perfect, the very reverse of such an act of complete omission. One can often see such an attempt at idealisation in the case of the male genitals in Greek art. Even pubic hair can have its idealised moment for the male. But the cunt is simply excised from the cultural record. Compare this approach with the beautifully observed realisation of the cunt in the art of Japan and its careful formalisation in the Kali Yantra in Indian art. By contrast, in classical art there is no attempt at anything or rather a concerted attempt at nothing. That is to say: a concerted attempt to not represent, not even to abstract. If the accounts are true, it confused Ruskin; it certainly confuses me. Where did the cunt go and why? A rhetorical question? Perhaps its answer, which I hope at least I approach, is related to the fact that one of the most beautiful of words in our language, 'cunt', is also deemed offensive. It is denied admittance to everyday polite discourse much as the physical form is denied admittance to classical sculpture or to printed media on public display; 'Eros denied', as Wayland Young put it.

Did that denial on Ruskin's part make him unable to participate honestly in that doctrine of truth to nature that his followers felt that he advocated? Although one does wonder what was meant by the words 'truth' and 'nature'. For Ruskin, the truth of Turner lay not in verisimilitude but in the exaggerations of what he called Turnerian topography. Japanese Shunga artists adopt a similar exaggerated approach to the genitals of both men and women in their erotic prints and drawings, in each case the aesthetic, the feeling, magnified to match psychological perception; just as it is in landscape for Turner in, for example, his small watercolour of Glencoe now in the possession of the Rhode Island School of Design.

Ruskin claimed to have destroyed a number of Turner's erotic drawings: was he worried that Turner was developing a visual grammar for what would have been a Western version of Shunga? Some of Turner's drawings suggest precisely that. So: Ruskin the iconoclast.

I owe Ruskin a debt for taking care of me in Venice, introducing me to the place. It was not, however, his images from *The Stones of Venice* that came to mind; rather, it was those of the first edition of *The Seven Lamps of Architecture* published in 1849 in which Ruskin etched the plates himself. Whatever the beauty of the versions later engraved by R. P. Cuff, they do not compete with the stark and energetic brilliance of Ruskin's own hand. His amateurish etching technique adds immediacy. He thought nothing of filling a hotel basin with acid to bite his plate while the subject was fresh in his mind. So it was examples of Ruskin's own work that were present to me as I found myself absorbed in the beauty of those weathered marble surfaces.

My battered copy of *The Seven Lamps* once belonged to a library more modest in scale than Venice's Biblioteca Marciana, but an equally civic place, a public library in a Scottish town on the edge of the North Sea, where a nineteenth century librarian had the good sense to back Ruskin's etchings with linen; as a result, the book survived a century and a half of public use before coming into my hands. The socialist in Ruskin would have been pleased that the people of Montrose wanted to read it and look at it time and time again.

Art is an exploration of where the virtual and the material become one. The human condition. The word incarnate. Information made physical. I value my own first edition of *The Seven Lamps of Architecture* for its materiality. I think myself into the rough detail of the dark spaces etched by Ruskin out of metal, so wild that they hardly hold the ink, and yet that very hint at instability is inherent to their aesthetic. And I value the materiality of the linen backing of the prints, and that this is indeed a library book, that most useful of material things. What completes the book for me is the bookplate. It has a motto from Virgil, in which the poet is referring to the attributes of the goddess Pheme or Fama, that is to say 'Fame', sometimes called 'Rumour'. According to Virgil: *Vires Acquirit Eundo,* 'She gathers strength as she goes'. Indeed so. A fuller version is: 'In the freedom of her movement is her power and she gathers new strength as she goes'. The rumour in question for Virgil was that Dido of Carthage and Aeneas of Troy had become lovers. As I hold the book in my hand I feel the irony of the fame of Ruskin and Effie as non-lovers, non-lovers at the time the book was published.

In the preface to a later edition Ruskin reflects on his etchings, valuing them highly and by contrast valuing Cuff's work only as 'quite as good for all practical illustration'. To anyone familiar with Cuff's superb versions of Ruskin's images that assessment may seem unduly disparaging yet that is not Ruskin's intention; indeed, if anyone has ever appreciated the art of the engraver it is Ruskin. Why then does Ruskin take the trouble to draw attention to his own etchings if for the purposes of illustrating his book Cuff had made such a good job of emulating them? The reason is that Ruskin knew in his heart that those etchings were among his finest achievements as an artist. In these few images made with as he puts it 'savage carelessness', we have Ruskin the true artist unleashed. The paradox is that their truth to Ruskin's nature is in conflict with his own declared aims. They are savagely careless, literally aesthetic, brimming with feeling. Yet 'aesthetic' was the very category Ruskin had rejected or rather, downgraded in his writing. That downgrade takes place at the beginning of the second volume of *Modern Painters*, published in 1846. He consigns the use of the word 'aesthesis' – reasonably enough, for that is what it implies – to sensual perception but for Ruskin this is 'mere' sensual perception and he goes on to 'wholly deny that the impressions of beauty are in any way sensual'. And that denial of the sensual is at the heart of the difficulty he faced in life.

For Ruskin to value so highly his savagely careless works, his sensual works, is revealing. Perhaps he was in love; certainly, this was the time of his marriage to Effie Gray. But at the time he should have been making love to her he seems to have forgotten the sensuousness of his etchings and tutored himself again in his desire to 'wholly deny that the impressions of beauty are in any way sensual'. He continues: 'they are neither sensual nor intellectual, but moral'. What he means by any of this, I do not know. The words seem to have meaning, but that meaning slips away. The main function of the words seems to be to separate the thinker from the world; or to put it another way, to rationalise the eternal separation of Ruskin from the object of his love whether that object is nature or Effie. By contrast, as the author of these etchings Ruskin becomes everything he thought he stood against. He lets himself feel. He lets himself become involved in the aesthetic and in the end, he cannot bring himself to reject that feeling in favour of his beloved non-sensuous alternative '*theoria*'. Nor could he fully accept that feeling, so this truth of his work is seen only in etchings that remain hidden in the first edition of *The Seven Lamps of Architecture* and their savage carelessness is not replicated elsewhere. Ruskin the almost-romantic. Ruskin the almost-lover. Ruskin the almost-Turner.

Must any thinker in any medium sacrifice a degree of sanity on some altar that they do not understand, in order to gain perspective? When he wrote of sacrifice was Ruskin implying the sacrifice of his own aesthetic, his own physical existence, his own feeling, to the ideas he felt he needed to control his thought? For Ruskin does write of sacrifice. Not the annual sacrifice of the young king which had inspired Turner's painting *The Golden Bough*, the work that would in due course be the starting point for James Frazer, but the sacrifice of time and skill in the crafting of detail that underpins the sense of the whole; the detail that is made beautiful by the intensity of art and craft but in principle need not and may never be seen. Why should that be so important? It is because that detail seen or unseen implies the whole just as the whole implies that detail. If a part implies completion when it is not in itself complete, then the whole is dishonest. That is the essence of Ruskin's mental ecology.

In Venice for Ruskin the detail of every capital, every marble surface implied the whole. Yet, like any other city, Venice was and is a city in evolution. Although it is seemingly trapped in time and by geography, it must continuously reinvent itself. A paradox of Ruskin is that he did not want Venice to reinvent itself and on that paradox, a further paradox is heaped. For Ruskin was drawn to that city by Turner, the very artist who had reinvented Venice more than any other before or since.

Does every insight or failure of such begin with a detail, or a detail missed or denied? Like the detail of Effie Gray that Ruskin was denying to himself, and thus not seeing the whole? The unseen? The implied? That aspect of women's beauty that Ruskin seems to have almost consciously sacrificed on the altars of those whom he most despised: the neo-classicists. 'The admiration of Canova I hold to be one of the most deadly symptoms in the civilization of the upper classes in the present century'. Yet it is Ruskin's own admiration for that neoclassical endorsement of the classical removal of the cunt—of which Canova was one of the greatest exponents—which lies at the heart of his inability to live up to his desire to be true to nature. For Ruskin, truth was literal. But Canova knew that art, like language, is provisional, a mode of expression made to meet necessity, and that part of that necessity is always the conventions, the mores, of the day. By comparison Ruskin regarded art and truth as in an absolute relation. The problem with such absolutism is that if it is not right in every detail—which it can never be—it leads to madness.

Or, as in Ruskin's case, it leads one to write a preface in which one acknowledges one's own 'savage carelessness'. Prefaces so often let the cat out the bag. 'Savage' is an interesting and misunderstood word. It does not mean uncultured; it means part of a culture which is still in touch with the wild. That is a very different thing. When Ernest Thompson Seton wrote his book *Two Little Savages* in 1903, the term was used in admiration of Dene culture, not as an insult to it, an attempt to learn from it, not to belittle it. In describing his own savage carelessness Ruskin felt the edge of his own unity with the wild through his art. It might seem ironic that this wildness in Ruskin emerges in response to that most civilised of skills, architecture. Yet that wildness gives the uneasy edge to all culture and without that uneasy edge, however enjoyable, culture becomes kitsch.

Alongside the cultured iconoclasm of Greek art is the wild reality of myth. How else could one create a goddess of love except in a sea boiling with blood and semen from the torn-off genitals of her father? Few images even hint at that primordial energy of Aphrodite. A drawing by Girodet edges in the right direction. And Oedipus's mother took him to bed and enjoyed him in gratitude, for he had saved her city, her civilised aspect; what else would she do? Apart from know herself, of course; and Oedipus came in due course to know himself, putting out his eyes by way of acknowledgment. In contrast Ruskin never knew himself and in that failure, he is kindred to me.

Was Ruskin so compelled by the Greek aesthetic that anything else was anathema? Did he feel that to accept a reality so far from the ancient Greek approach would have destroyed him, so instead did he allow his willing misconception to destroy him in another way, by destroying his own sexuality?

A curiosity of the Greek response is that the beautiful swelling of the mound of Venus is fully captured, but all else is denied as though it had never existed. Maybe that was the point, for the classical Greek culture to which we pay so much heed—for it is indeed our own—is an incomplete, masculinist re-mythologising of earlier goddess myths. What better way to hide the mythology than to imply the genitals of the goddess but to negate them. This is a seeming acknowledgment when there is, in fact, none. Everywhere the goddess becomes downplayed to become a mere bit part in the story of the gods. Pasiphae is downgraded to become the accidental mother of a monster, rather than a goddess who requires the power of a sacred bull to satisfy her. The intelligence of Ariadne simply leads to her abandonment. Something of the earlier goddess survives here and there as when, as Titian understood, Diana unmasters the hounds of Actaeon's desire and makes of him a sacrifice.

At the same time a little further east, the finding of knowledge courtesy of Eve is defined as the first sin, whatever that may be, and the originality of her discovery is not just devalued but seen as negative. From another point of view the myth reads differently as the sacred serpent of the goddess makes knowledge available to a woman and through her to the first man. In reward for its role the serpent leaves the tree of knowledge, its task done, and is reunited with the goddess's fertile earthly body. There is a drawing by Rodin depicting Minerva that catches the sense of this. His sculpture of Eve is more subdued. Only occasionally, as in Suzanne Valadon's naked self-portrait with her lover, does Eve get truer representation.

The genital mutilation of women in art carries on through the rediscovery of the presumed accurate art of the Greeks and Romans in the Renaissance into Ruskin's own times, for example, Hiram Powers's sculpture *Greek Slave Girl* from 1844 or Ingres's painting *La Source* (begun in Rome in 1820 but not completed until 1856) among much else. Then in 1866, seventeen years after the publication of Ruskin's savagely careless etchings in *The Seven Lamps of Architecture*, Courbet's wild but carefully painted *L'Origine du monde* took a more sensible path. That this painting is still controversial says much about Ruskin's difficulty, not only with respect to his own uneasiness, but that uneasiness as part of a continuum of Western everyday denial of a reality of women.

That continuity of denial was confronted with elegance by the performance artist Deborah de Robertis in 2014. De Robertis took Courbet's image a step further by opening her cunt in the presence of the painting. The true artist is one who can take that one step further, not for the sake of innovation, but for the sake of truth. Courbet did that in 1866. De Robertis did that in 2014. As Collingwood writes: 'The artist must prophesy not in the sense that he foretells things to come, but in the sense that he tells his audience, at the risk of their displeasure, the secrets of their own hearts'. There are no better examples of that than Courbet on the one hand and De Robertis on the other. It is something of an irony that Collingwood's father was Ruskin's secretary.

The gesture made by De Robertis is one of the oldest gestures a woman can make, and in the West at least, except in the Sheela na Gig tradition, the most taboo. Taboo: a word that the Imperial anthropologists of Ruskin's day imported—with glee concealed as academic fervor—into the languages of the West, to reveal the 'strange' aspects of 'savage' behaviour, which they so deeply desired. Both Courbet and De Robertis insist on breaking the Western taboo of close observation of the cunt but with a very Ruskinian attention to detail, the detail that makes the whole possible. The detail of Proust's madeleine. The instant of taste and sight and smell that creates human history. That attention to detail is why Proust loved Ruskin so. A *petite madeleine*, a sunned panel of marble, the beauty revealed when a woman opens herself to her lover, or—as a performance artist—to the world.

There is a theory in physics that the universe was created by a fluctuation from nothing. The first detail. The first thought. The first step. The first memory. The first taste. The first gesture. When Heraclitus said that he could not step into the same river twice, he noted the importance of such detail in time. In Tantric cosmology, two is but a fluctuation of one, and when the two primordial lovers separate, the womb of the cosmos gives birth to all things. There is an image of the entrance to that cosmic womb by Hildegard of Bingen that dates from the twelfth century; one can interpret it both as a vulva and an illumination of the almond shape (mandorla) created by the intersection of two circles, a symbol of unity of logos and material, of immortal and mortal, and valued as such by medieval Christians. It is echoed in the floor plan of Chartres. It is echoed as a garland in the card that expresses 'The World' in the Tarot de Marseilles. In his *Lectures on Landscape* given to his Oxford students in 1871 Ruskin illustrated the form as it is found in the west front of Dunblane Cathedral, describing it as 'one of the prettiest pieces of rough thirteenth century carving in the kingdom'. Ruskin edges towards the beauty of the cunt but always by proxy. One of the most vulva-like of all his drawings is, appropriately enough, an aerial view of the Holy Land.

Why could Ruskin not tolerate the beauty of the cunt? Was he shocked by its leaf-like crenulations and flower-like detail? Did he expect the entrance to the womb to be a thing of no consequence? He would have drawn it superbly, as did Turner. Another of Ruskin's drawings comes to mind. He draws a cleft of rock filled with wild strawberries. Was he aware of the immense sensuality of his image? Perhaps on a conscious level he was not and yet he was a deeply sensual man. What he lacked was the ability to make of his intellect and his sensuality one thing. And that is the task that we all face; to make the word incarnate, so to speak. To admit that we are physical beings coded and coding in time, and that time is itself physical. The body and breath of God. The life and soul of the party.

How can the word be incarnate? Perhaps it is just a question of noticing. But Ruskin searched for what he already believed. And when he confronted what he thought unbelievable, not morally possible to believe, like the genitals of a woman or the erotic drawings of Turner, he denied and destroyed. For in order to draw the cunt he had to admit it existed. But if he admitted it existed he had to admit that the art history of the West was based on the fraudulent imagery of the Greeks. That should not have been so difficult for Ruskin, critical as he was of the dominance of classicism, but at the same time he accepted the classical world's value as a point of origin of Western thought and there is a consistency in Ruskin which I admire. It led him to accept the art of that classical world over life itself.

For Ruskin, truth to nature had its limits. In the end, nature had to conform to the history of Western art. If he admitted the existence of the cunt he had to deny that history. And that he could not do. So instead he denied the truth of the cunt. And as a result of that denial he insisted that his hero Turner should posthumously deny it too. So Ruskin, *via* the iconoclasm of the ancient Greek mind—if we are to believe his own account—became himself that tawdry thing, an iconoclast. And his desire to be true to nature became for a moment no more than prejudice.

Far from art being true to nature, for Ruskin it was true to morality, a changing set of *mores*, mistaken to be eternal. When Marcel Proust grappled with this he had to move on from Ruskin. That Ruskin was such an influence on Proust is an index of his cultural reach and it is a reminder that although I might seem to criticise Ruskin, I do so only because he stands in for myself. Proust moved on, and perhaps I too move on, not because Ruskin was wrong but because whether he was right or wrong depends not on art but on morality. The curious thing is that the roots of morality lie in relativism. Why is a word that simply implies 'customary' used to imply some kind of quasi-absolute value for certain behaviours? Not that I would wish to deny all universalism. When Iseult questions Tristram's reticence he replies, with a morality that has a hint of the universal, 'ask the custom'.

The inherent relativism of morality is a problem for Ruskin, although he does not admit or even know it. Truth to nature may have been a plausible notion. The idea that such truth could have any correspondence to the changing customs that underpin morality was simply a non-starter.

Novalis writes: 'What is nature? An encyclopaedic, systematic index or plan of our spirit'. Blake writes: 'Nature has no outline but imagination has'. They are both right, for we feel our way as beings both towards constructing the world and having the world construct us. We are on that edge; that edge where the word becomes incarnate; where the information is physical. In the beginning was not so much the word as the untranslatable Greek term 'logos' – as much image as word. In the beginning was the calligraphy, the ideogram, the gesture. There is a translation of the beginning of St John's Gospel that eschews 'word' in favour of 'logos'. In the beginning was the logos. The discourse. The text. The textile. The woven thing. The knot. The narrative. And it is in the Latin form, *verbum*, that we find the word standing in as best it can for logos and made truly incarnate by inscription on vellum by a monk of Iona. What was in the mind of the artist as his steady hand and heart delineated some of the most beautiful patterns ever conceived? Perhaps he was concentrating on making the word physical, beautiful. 'Perhaps' is a word that opens doors and leaves doors open. Ruskin became an iconoclast when he rejected those openings. 'Perhaps I am wrong' is the deepest of conscious truths. For the iconoclast, there is no 'perhaps'.

Did Ruskin feel relief as Turner's erotic art burned in front of him? Or did he simply claim that he burned it and feel the relief of his lie? Nothing with Ruskin is ever simple. Either way I think he felt only his own suffering. Perhaps he felt nothing for to suffer is to allow—to bear—and Ruskin could not bear Turner being himself. Ruskin required conformity. But the conformity he required was not to the received wisdom of the day or even to the actual wisdom of Turner but conformity to his own view. It is a paradox that this made him a great critic able to break and remake the mould of criticism. His pioneering work was called *Modern Painters* and he was the first modern critic, the first truly independent critical voice. He forced change.

He changed the way we think about art and life, but he could not change himself.

Some accounts have suggested that it was Effie's lack of conformity to Ruskin's moral expectations rather than her sexual presence that Ruskin could not bear. Perhaps. Years later would the teenage Rose La Touche have conformed to his moral expectations? Perhaps. Would Rose and Ruskin have fucked if she had accepted his proposal of marriage? Perhaps. Did Effie and Ruskin ever fuck? Perhaps. All that is really known is that when Effie left Ruskin for Millais, Effie and Millais fucked a lot. They had eight children. If Ruskin fucked at all, he didn't fuck much. But he did his best to love. In 1860 he wrote, in *Unto This Last*: 'There is no wealth but life. Life, including all its powers of love, of joy, and of admiration'. Like much of his writing it is a bit of a sermon (and becomes even more so) but he meant it, and it transformed people, and it still does. It may be the writing of a failed lover but it is the writing of a generous soul; a generous soul who still wanted to marry, even if he did not have much of a clue. Six years later he proposed to Rose La Touche. That same year, 1866, Courbet painted *L'Origine du monde*.

Like a Tantric thought, to what did Courbet's image give birth? For me, it gives birth to Proust, the writer who took art as his way into the world and Ruskin as his guide. There is a class of book that eludes easy definition because the balance between verbal and visual is so notably achieved. The first edition of *The Seven Lamps of Architecture* is one such book. Another is Eric Karpeles's *Paintings in Proust*. Layers of critical varnish are removed by the simple device of remaking the novel for the reader through the art to which Proust refers. Through those images the weave goes back and forth between Proust and Ruskin.

A surprising proportion of words that deal with abstract thought have their origin in the visual or the kinaesthetic. 'Theory' for example. Or 'abstract'. Logos, however, has no such etymology. For logos means nothing, in the most positive sense of non-sense, non-meaning. It takes its place with other words which one might call meta-semantic. 'God' is one such word. Where nothing and everything are without distinction. 'Logos' is that which, with Wittgenstein or Shakespeare, we may decide to pass over in silence. It is what, with Borges we may discover in the accumulation of disorder in the attic. For Hildegard of Bingen, it is the feather on the breath of God. For the Anglo-Saxon poet of Ruthwell, it is the dream of the rood. If it has any equivalent in English it is that strange process word which we tend to take for granted, so much so that we behave as if it existed: 'time' and all that it implies. Memory, for example. *À la recherche du temps perdu*. Or, as Shakespeare put it: 'remembrance of things past'.

What might that mean? Borges, translated by Alistair Reid, writes: 'To forgetting, to all forgotten objects I have just erected this monument / (Unquestionably less durable than bronze) which will be lost among them'. Perhaps it means something like that. Or like this: 'To reach it, a ladder has to be set up. There is no stair. / What can we be looking for in the attic / but the accumulation of disorder?'. Borges again, earlier in the same poem. Freud might have described that accumulation of order or disorder as symptomatic of the 'uneasiness inherent in culture'. Bettelheim reminds us of the spin put on Freud by his translators: 'civilization and its discontents'. How neat and conjunctive. No inherent uneasiness there. Just some discontents that can no doubt be sorted out with a little common sense. Like the everyday problems of Empire.

Proust, like Freud, like Ruskin, lived in co-relation to the old European empires trying to renew themselves across the globe in the traditional manner. Like Ruskin, like any of us, he had to work out how to avoid colluding in the ornamentalist silliness of it all, if at all possible. It is too simple to say that if you avoid kitsch you avoid empire but it is a good start. It is more accurate to say that while kitsch does not necessarily imply empire it is one of its accompaniments. In 1877, six years after Proust was born, a British queen was declared Empress of India. At that moment the British Empire reinvented the monarch as kitsch. In the same year Proust's hero Whistler sued Proust's other hero Ruskin, and the world of art and life turned on a farthing's damages. It was a year of small-mindedness under the guise of great issues. An empress for India? A pot of paint thrown in the face of the public? A farthing's damages for being stupidly right? Some old deity would have been laughing. Poor Victoria. A genuine person, attempting like Ruskin to love people but caught up in the kitsch of politics. Did she ever fuck John Brown? I hope so. Or if not him, someone else. She deserved a bit of the companionship of good sex after the sadness of losing Albert.

It is interesting that Roland Barthes's exploration of an image of John and Victoria together is not informed by the potentially erotic relationship between them. The photograph was taken about two years after Albert's death. Barthes's knowledge may have been circumscribed but with intuitive synchrony he writes in the very next paragraph of an image by Robert Mapplethorpe: 'The erotic photograph [...] takes the photograph outside its frame'. Is that not what all framed works do? The frame seems to bind the image; in fact, it allows it to take its place, to take the viewer into its place. The viewer is taken in by the image and takes in the image. Within the frame, that non-dimensional thing, one meets (or does not meet) oneself.

Good art always surprises. It surprises because one thought one knew it as an old friend or enemy but one did not. It always has the capacity to shock; it is always somehow experientially raw. One of the very worst, most dislikable of Venetian artists is

Tiepolo. A mere virtuoso, until one is shocked by his brilliance of self-effacement, and suddenly he becomes part of one's thought, instead of a figure to be dismissed. Roberto Calasso's *Tiepolo Pink* helped me to see Tiepolo properly. Suddenly, shockingly, Tiepolo was no longer caught in a cul-de-sac of technique but became the herald of Goya. Tiepolo is the artist within whom reason begins to sleep and dream fitfully. That is most evident in his etchings, his *Capricci* and *Scherzi*. Like those of Ruskin, they have an element of savage carelessness that inflects with shadow the memory of his radiant paintings

In Padua, I lived in Via Giovanni Battista Tiepolo. I am glad of that address. From my studio with its sun and trees and rooftops moderated by early morning mist it was a rewarding walk to the libraries through intelligently arcaded streets. Close to my route were places about which Ruskin had written. Months before I had dug out my old pocket edition of his account of Giotto's frescoes in the Arena chapel. When I had time, I paid them a visit but the chapel had become a shrine in thrall to its air conditioning. I prefer to remember the work as I first encountered it in a book published by Hallwag of Berne in 1969. The chapel is itself something of an artist's book in architectural form: I was happy enough to return to it as a book, the reproductions more real for me than the reality.

Proust explored the expanded field of visual art that photographic and lithographic reproduction made possible. For him, Giotto's work could be a reproduction hanging on the wall of a French schoolroom. Walter Benjamin and, following him, John Berger reflected on such copies and the consequent loss of 'aura' of the original. But for Proust, and for me, there is only the gain of imagining oneself where one wants to be despite the inevitability of the storm from paradise, whether it is that of Klee or of Giorgione. In another part of the storm the old poet Borges gropes for a book in his library: 'And the city, now, is like a map / Of my humiliations and failures; / From this door, I have seen the twilights / And at this marble pillar I have waited in vain'. Who translated that? Where did I find it? Ruskin is less elegant in his distress. He wrote in 1858:

> Indeed I rather want good wishes just now for I am tormented by what I cannot get said, nor done. I want to get all the Titians, Tintorets, Paul Veroneses, Turners and Sir Joshuas in the world into a great fireproof Gothic gallery of marble and serpentine. I want to get them all engraved. I want to go and draw all of the subjects of Turner's 19,000 sketches in Switzerland and Italy, elaborated by myself. I want to get everybody a dinner who hasn't got one. I want to macadamise some new roads to heaven with broken fools heads [...] I want to play all day long and arrange my cabinet of minerals with new white wool. I want Turner's pictures not

> to fade – I want to be able to draw clouds [...] and I can't do anything and don't understand what I was born for [...].

He has my sympathy. Ruskin was a prosaic man. He did not, could not, transcend. Or am I writing about myself? In an attempt to transcend prose at least I am tempted to call Ruskin 'mosaic' rather than prosaic. For like Ruskin, I want to play: and this one word is in fact two, one that means pertaining to the muses (as in mosaic floor) and the other that means pertaining to Moses (as in Mosaic law). Like Ruskin, Freud embodied both meanings as he sat in his temple of the muses first in Vienna and then in London, a true Moses who could never enter the Promised Land, for he understood more than anyone that it was and is an illusion. Freud's study is a museum in the real sense of a place that welcomes in the muses. That is a dangerous thing to do. Some museums try to contain the threat. Others let the muses fly furious and free. That beautiful, Ruskin-inspired confection of order, the Oxford Museum, conceals, as if behind a screen, the fabulous anti-Ruskinian proto-chaos of the Pitt Rivers. In the outer museum, everything is in its place. Entering the Pitt Rivers, the world – the word – becomes arbitrary, a moving, weaving, different sort of thing, no longer in one's capacity to define.

Prosaic Ruskin had a transcendent twin in George Frederick Watts. I realise now that many of the small halftone reproductions that introduced me to the imagery of Greek myth were based on paintings by Watts: Ariadne, Eve, Orpheus, Eurydice, the Minotaur, Europa; and later in sculptural form Clytie the nymph who—as lovers must—always inclines to her beloved. Watts was born in 1817, two years before Ruskin, and he died four years after him, in 1904. Both men had lives close in date to Victoria. We should allow Victoria to be part of the Ruskinian age rather than *vice versa*. It would give us more purchase on making sense of her as a person. Watts and Ruskin had curiously cognate relationships with women, which had notably different outcomes. Both attempted to marry twice. Both married Scots once (as Victoria is reputed to have done also). Both loved women much younger than themselves. The differences are, however, marked. Where Ruskin's Scottish love simply revealed his own inadequacy, naivety, morality or whatever one wishes to call it, and brought to him as little happiness as he brought to her, Watts's Scottish love gave an extraordinary stability to the final chapter of his creative life, and at the same time complemented his art with her own, in a way that is still not fully appreciated. Mary Fraser Tytler was born in India in 1849 and returned to her family home beside Loch Ness at the age of two. In due course, she made a unique contribution to the Celtic revival at Compton in the heart of the Home Counties of England. I arrived by chance at the chapel, cloister, and garden that she had designed, a garden of graves in which the dead rest easy, and it is through her care for the dead that we can understand her care for the living. It is a place of visionary art and craft where the designs of Iona and Islay—remade for a new age—find their way into the Surrey hills.

A sense of her can be found in her book *The Word in the Pattern*, the logos, so to speak. Was it the logos that her husband tried to paint in his late works? That is as good an explanation as any. There is a tending to non-figurative space. It is not abstract, for it is an attempt to represent not to abstract from representation. Mondrian abstracted; Watts did not. But they both approached a beyond-figurative space in order to transcend. A transcendence both formal and spiritual. Claude does the same thing. He is often thought of as if he were an intellectually poor relation to Poussin, but Poussin was simply a more obvious artist in his pursuit of visual thinking. Claude was—like Watts, like Mondrian—treading the edge of being in form, the transcendental edge. The liminal space or process in which flesh becomes word, incarnate becomes logos.

Claude's *Psyche Outside the Castle of Cupid* from 1664 is one such liminal space; with its evening glow, it is almost a Watts. Claude's *Landscape with Ascanius Shooting the Stag of Sylvia* from 1682, with its strongly stated geometry, is almost a Mondrian. Why did Ruskin so object to Claude when his hero Turner rated him so highly? It is simple enough. Claude constructed his pictures from natural elements with no pretence that his landscapes as a whole were true to nature, except in some idealised sense. Such constructivism was not acceptable to Ruskin. Art, for Ruskin, could not simply be true to itself. Ruskin would have found Mondrian's work equally distressing. But for Turner Claude constructed images that are containers of light, and for Turner, that was the real truth of nature. For those two artists light was 'real with the most real reality', to paraphrase William James.

The paradox is that Ruskin, Turner's greatest admirer, tried to tie Turner back to the earth, while Turner was always rising from it with the light. Ruskin understood this to a degree, wondering at and imitating Turner's paintings of clouds, but in the end for him Turner's power was as a painter of location, of the specific. 'I want to go and draw all of the subjects of Turner's 19,000 sketches in Switzerland and Italy, elaborated by myself'. Turner, despite or because of his ability to paint locality, was in the end a painter who made of the substance of paint the infinite, who made of the material the logos.

I had brought with me to Venice a postcard of a watercolour by Turner: an image of the Piazzetta illuminated by a lightning strike. The original can be found in the Vaughan Bequest to the National Gallery of Scotland. Yet it was not the transcendence of Turner that saved me in St Mark's Square but Ruskin's attention to detail. Although initially I saw the square through Ruskin's etchings I found myself appreciating the detail of his work in a different medium. Ruskin picked up quickly on the then newly perfected technique of photography and he well understood the value of the daguerreotype as a way of imaging architecture. Daguerreotypes have a density of detail and a visual flatness that can distract from a portrait of a person, but which can only add to an understanding of architecture. Ruskin's daguerreotypes of Venice illuminate his architectural subjects. While he toiled over his pioneering, precise, and insightful photographs, Effie was enjoying the city in an altogether more relaxed manner. Venice needed them both; he to record architecture in every detail, she to become part of the sensual lifeblood of the place. It is fitting that they were both so suited to that city, for a city must comprehend such plurality.

Architectural photography begins with Ruskin. I do not mean simply taking a picture of a building. William Henry Fox Talbot did that very effectively—and beautifully—with some of his first calotypes. Ruskin's daguerreotypes were taken in order to better understand a building, tools to make every possible detail of the architecture available for later consideration. There are images made by Ruskin and his assistant John Hobbs that have a particular significance for me for they were made in locations close to the spot where I began to see Venice through Ruskin's eyes. They were taken in

1849 or 1850 from the balcony of the Doge's Palace. One, with the camera positioned at the corner of the balcony closest to St Mark's, was used by Ruskin as a guide for a drawing of the southwest detail of the basilica, complete with the upper part of one of the St Jean d'Acre columns in the foreground. That very corner where Ruskin set up his camera is critical also to Turner's Piazzetta composition, anchoring the background by implication, as the column of St Theodore anchors the foreground. Both Turner and Ruskin understood the complexity of the Piazzetta as emblematic of the complexity of Venice.

Another Ruskin daguerreotype shows a wider view. It was made from further along the balcony and includes part of the north side of the piazza as well as the corner of the basilica. This panorama has at its core another of the elements that saved Venice for me: a twenty-four-hour analogue clock dating from the fifteenth century. 'Analogue' twelve-hour clocks are not really analogue at all. In cosmic terms the hands progress twice as fast as they should. By comparison there is something steadfast about the true analogue progression of a twenty-four-hour clock, which precisely reflects the speed of rotation of the planet with respect to the sun. Most of these clocks take that further by also showing the position of the sun in the zodiac. On my first evening in Padua I had seen such a twenty-four-hour clock in the Piazza dei Signori. Later I came across one integrated into Pietro d'Abano's scheme of astrological murals in the Palazzo della Ragione. Pietro's scheme was inspired in large measure by the earlier thinking of Michael Scot and it was first given painted form by Pietro's contemporary Giotto. That first visualisation was destroyed by fire in 1420. The current version restores the fifteenth century work of Nicolò Miretto, Stefano da Ferrara, and others, that was itself damaged after most of the roof was ripped off by a tornado in 1756. Despite its vicissitudes, Pietro's scheme in its three hundred and thirty-three panels survives and enchants.

Astrology does not fit with our dominant worldview because it evades causality. Yet as the behaviour of matter under quantum conditions is understood as similarly evasive to causal explanation, other ways of seeing should be given more leeway, not as alternatives to scientific method and insight but as necessary echoes of something or other.

Jung notes a system of engaging in a non-causal manner, one developed in China several thousand years ago. *I Ching: The Book of Changes* was translated by his friend, the missionary Richard Wilhelm. It is said to be one of the great translations, and readers of it in English (such as I) think of it as such. Of course we do not know, for we are reading it not in Wilhelm's German, but in the translation of his words by Cary Baynes. What we know is that Baynes's work is one of the great translations. One might think that such translation upon translation would distance the reader too much from the original. Yet the curious thing about the *I Ching* is that it has no original from which to be distanced and that is its point. It has an idea, which seems to be a good one, and that is bounded and defined. It has commentaries and these are endless. Every translation or translation of a translation adds to those commentaries. Some of those commentaries have little value though all, however inept, have some value. Some, like the Baynes translation of Wilhelm, move things forward for the reader and do so every time they are opened. Jung thought of consulting the *I Ching* as like looking at one's watch, but in a cosmic sense. That gets something of it. Jung's friend Hermann Hesse wrote of it as a work that 'I shall never be able to understand except intuitively and for moments'. I first encountered it through Hesse's novel, *The Glass Bead Game*. Hesse continues: 'this is not reading or thinking, but it is like looking into the flowing water or drifting clouds. Everything is written there that can be thought and lived'.

Is everything that can be thought and lived painted on the walls of the Palazzo della Ragione in Padua? That is one way of looking at it or at least of attempting to understand its intent. But that cycle of imagery is far from the only interest that the building holds. The roof is a kind of inverted ship's hull, allowing the space below to be uninterrupted by even a single column. That space is about ninety yards long and thirty yards wide. It is Europe's first truly modern covered space, predating the great exhibition halls of London and Paris by half a millennium. Ruskin drew the arcaded exterior, but not the interior. Was he simply horrified by its radical architectural purity? Nothing could be less like the Oxford Museum, which for all its nineteenth-century ironwork is deliberately and beautifully cluttered with stone columns and capitals.

Yet the Palazzo della Ragione is also a museum, for covering every inch of its walls is that elaboration of the cosmos and the seasons, and the assertion of the nature of justice and change. It is the book of the Comune di Padova: hall of reason, hall of justice, hall of contract, hall of meeting, the place that enabled the city to be a city. The murals have a lightness of touch yet their imagery adds presence to every activity that has ever taken place there, even—perhaps most of all—to the wanderings of the curious tourist, pilgrim, or refugee.

At one end of that hall is a sculpture of a horse. It was once attributed to Donatello, and certainly relates in form to the horse of his Gattamelata monument, also in Padua. But this vast wooden horse holds its own, and more so, as a sculptural object. Anything less than a hall of the scale of the Palazzo della Ragione would cramp it. If Ruskin saw it was he offended by the truth to nature of its substantial bollocks? If Effie was with him she would no doubt have been intrigued. Her testament was life where his was only wondering about life. Effie might, however, have been less than impressed by the average Renaissance treatment of the genitals of the human male. Donatello's *David* is no match for that horse. Perhaps one can understand the ancient Greek model used by Renaissance artists not as prudish *per se* but as minimising the sexual charge that imagery of the genitals tends to conjure for the viewer in favour of a focus on beauty of proportion, just as one might understand Japanese Shunga artists as maximising imagery of the genitals in favour of focus on the beauty of sensation. Both approaches have their validity. The modesty of Donatello's *David* or Cellini's *Perseus* on the one hand and on the other Utamaro's topography—Turnerian in spirit—of lovemaking. Yet Utamaro, when the mood takes him, is also the most subtle of artists, every bit as concerned with proportion above all as an ancient Greek. In that mood Utamaro is like Tiepolo. They are both elegant and discreet, yet in their discretion everything is implied. They lived in different halves of the same century at different ends of the by-then unravelling silk road, reminding us that Japan and Venice are like twins separated at birth, fostered to enable East and West respectively to understand the nature of art and ritual. Yet when the great exchange of the nineteenth century took place, Japan's art revolutionised the West, and Venice's finery was forgotten for a moment. But not by Proust, nor by his Japanese contemporary Okakura Kakuzo, who writes that 'there is no single recipe for making the perfect tea, as there are no rules for producing a Titian or a Sesson'. No rules, no recipe. Zen; the *logos*. Okakura spent much of his life in Boston, the city that did so much to make possible the rethink of the relation between the art of East and West; before Okakura through Fenollosa, after him, through Coomaraswamy. Yet it is the thinkers of Boston's hinterland that make the thought of that city, almost despite themselves. Thoreau most of all. 'In wildness is the preservation of the world'. The nature-tectonic giving context to the architectonic. A narrative of the need for Ruskin's savage carelessness that touches our wild reality.

Returning to this essay to edit it, I wonder what it is about. Is what I have written any more than an epigraph? A sort of lintel? I find myself in memory on a northern stair of the British Museum, looking at a painting of a torrent pouring down a cliff. It dates from 1992 and it is by the Japanese artist Konno Chuichi. Here is the deep north of Bashō; it is Yamagata province, or, as one might translate it, the Highlands. Museums are made by what one comes across by chance. The British Museum's character depends not on famous bits and pieces but on discoveries on stairwells, in basements. A coffer ceiling from a Greek temple. Or the gift of a Japanese painter. Konno's work recalls James Macpherson: 'The torrent pours down the rock. No hut receives me from the rain; forlorn on the hill of winds'. Perhaps one could rewrite *Ossian* in Haiku form. Goethe, in the person of Werther, translated that passage. The same words were set to music by James Oswald, the re-maker for the eighteenth century of the Aeolian Harp. There is a passage in Macpherson in which Ossian hangs his harp on the branch of an oak tree; he will never play it again. The strings stir in the breeze—and both tradition and art are validated by nature.

In 1797, around the time Turner was first imagining Italy in his paintings, Napoleon brought the history of the Venetian Republic to an abrupt close. He proceeded to loot the city—an activity very much in the spirit of that place. Was it among his new acquisitions that Napoleon first encountered the poems of Ossian? I think he knew them already. It was an Italian translation written in Venice—that of Cesarotti—that Napoleon took on his campaigns. The particular edition he carried with him is in three volumes published in Nice in 1780. Sturdy compact books, made for the traveller. When I first flipped one open I was startled by a bright field of experimental colour. The sheer presence of that marbled paper conveyed the book to me as a material thing, a work of visual art. Such endpapers are covers within covers, thresholds of the text block.

Did such art calm Napoleon's thinking as he advanced on Moscow? Or was he just interested in the heroism and deceit recounted in the text? By then he had commissioned Ossianic subjects from the painters Girodet and Gérard for Malmaison, and from Ingres for his palace in Rome. By then Ossian had reinvigorated the literature of Europe via Cesarotti and Goethe. The latter claimed sweeping passages of Macpherson's words for the dramatic culmination of his novel *The Sufferings of Young Werther*, published in 1774, and Werther was to penetrate European culture as deeply as would Ossian. At first that dual influence seems to culminate in opera in the late nineteenth century and yet the person of Werther resurfaces, and tellingly so, in Roland Barthes's *Fragments d'un discours amoureux*, published in 1977. In his title, was Barthes echoing Macpherson's *Fragments of Ancient Poetry*? Probably not, but both were writing in times of dissolution, post-conflict creative periods before the old empires consolidated their ideological grip once more. '*Toute mon âme est là*' sings Werther in Massenet's opera of 1887. Barthes writes that 'it is the amorous subject who, at a certain moment, departs'. Massenet's aria is a prelude to that departure. The place in which Werther finds his soul is his own translation of Ossian: '*Pourquoi me réveiller?*'. Tracking it back the phrase survives intact in Massenet's librettists *via* Goethe's German to Macpherson's 'why dost thou awake me?'.

In Macpherson's original the awakening is that of a flower not by the breath of spring—as Goethe translates it—but by a gale. Perhaps Goethe is right in the sense of his translation and Macpherson's gale is indeed intended to be gentle, as in Felicia Heman's 'when Spring's first gale / Comes forth to whisper where the violets lie', or John Keble's 'Softer than gale at morning prime'. In any case the warrior-bard Ossian takes this awakening as a meditation on his own death: 'To-morrow shall the traveller come; he that saw me in my beauty shall come. His eyes will search the field, but they will not find me'. Macpherson, introducing the Romantic Age, called it 'the joy of grief'. A century earlier, Bashō had written: 'The summer grasses / Are all that remain to us / Of warrior dreams'.

The warrior dreamers of Macpherson's childhood were his fellow Highlanders. At the Battle of Culloden in 1746 one army wore clothing made of a variety of intricately coloured woven textiles. The other army wore a uniform of red coats. The uniforms won, and the complexities of Scottish Highland Gaelic culture have been unravelling ever since. If this brings to mind the plot of Hollywood's *The Last Samurai*, why should it not? The dynamics are not dissimilar. Some Highlanders, like some Samurai took the government side, but all Highlanders, like all Samurai, regardless of their allegiance, suffered in the aftermath. That aftermath began when Macpherson was eleven years old. The first requirement was that his kinsfolk should remove their clothing and dress in a manner that had no significance for them, to dress as though they were prisoners in their own land.

The clothing they were required to remove was tartan. It is an interesting fabric, which is defined by internal visual rhyme. A piece of tartan is produced when an order of coloured threads is set up on a loom. This 'sett' of the tartan is repeated both in the warp and weft of the fabric; that is to say, if we were looking at it as if it were a painting on the wall, both vertically and horizontally. The size of each area of colour is specified by the number of threads. Tartan is, therefore, a fabric in which complexity is generated from a simple order of colours and gathering of threads. The weaving process itself expresses the idea. In this way, it differs from, say, a knotted carpet from Iran or Turkey or Afghanistan in which the purpose of the knotting is to depict a design, a Tree of Life or an American drone, for example. The process of weaving is driven by an image that has nothing to do with the weaving process itself. Each knot is a pixel: so much so that it even becomes possible to sign the work, as in the Ardabil Carpet in the Victoria and Albert Museum in London. The poet Gael Turnbull translated that signature thus: 'I, Maksoud / of Kashan, a slave, / wove this carpet / and these words / into the pattern, / tied each thread / with a knot — / four hundred, / less a score, / width of a thumb — / for thirty-seven years / till it was done / upon this floor / where you kneel'. By contrast, in the case of tartan the process is the pattern. The two are one and the same, there is no adjustment, no accommodation. The medium cannot be distinguished from the message. Tartan thus has both a post-McLuhan radicality and a pre-McLuhan integrity. Perhaps that is why tartan has been so beloved by designers of focal significance such as Alexander McQueen and Vivienne Westwood.

Artists have found similar value in it. The painter Richard Dunn gave perspective on that plural aesthetic in his tartan-minimalist transformation of the Edinburgh gallery Sleeper in 2009, *A Plaid Found at Culloden*. It invoked the form of late Mondrian and yet it was culturally an echo of conflict. Tartan is an echo, woven. Like a fractal, it builds itself up through reflections and repetitions of itself. The culture of Gaelic Scotland is deeply concerned with such reverberation of information, expressed in interlace, music, and song as well as in tartan. Or in the rhyme schemes of classical Gaelic poetry where end rhymes are complemented, like strands of colour, by the echoes of internal rhyme.

I wonder if Mary Somerville wore tartan in Venice? She writes: 'In crossing the Piazza San Marco, an acquaintance, who accompanied us, took us to [...] hear an echo'. She continues: 'I like an echo; yet there is something so unearthly about the aerial voice, that it never ceases to raise a superstitious chill in me, such as I have felt more than once as I read Ossian while travelling among our Highland hills in my early youth'. Finally: 'In one of the grand passes of the Oberland, when we were in Switzerland, we were enveloped in mist, through which peaks were dimly seen. We stopped to hear an echo; the response came clear and distinct from a great distance, and I felt as if the Spirit of the Mountain had spoken'. Did she write with her friend Turner in mind? He certainly shared her interest in Ossian. They also saw eye to eye on the interplay of science and art. When Turner painted his first Ossian work in 1802 he had not met Mary Somerville, and I am not clear when that meeting took place, but if she saw his painting from 1832 of the island of Staffa and Fingal's Cave she would have felt again the Ossianic frisson of her childhood. Fingal's Cave is not so much an echo chamber as a place of intense reverberation of both sound and light. Even on a calm day the sonority of the sea is palpable.

In Greek mythology Echo is personified as a mountain nymph; in the Gaelic language of Macpherson this infinite repeating sound is not a nymph but a son; not any son, but the son (*mac*) of the rock (*talla*). Or the son of the hall. *Talla*: Hall; Court; Rock; Cleft of a rock; Tower. *Talla nan sian*, the hall of storms; *mac-talla, or mac-talla nan creag*, the echo; *talla a' chiùil*, the music-hall. So Edward Dwelly tells us. Did Turner ever paint anything other than echoes, reverberations of light?

I would like to hear Mary Somerville's echo in Venice. Or her *mac-talla* in the Swiss mountains. Moorland is different. Culloden has no echo; indeed, it is as though all sound has been leached from the air. Tennyson would have understood: 'And so there grew great tracts of wilderness, / Wherein the beast was ever more and more, / But man was less and less, till Arthur came'. Yet if I am wrong and there is an echo it is also as Tennyson imagined it: 'And Echo there, whatever is ask'd her, answers "Death"'. As I live longer I reject Tennyson less.

There are places that one comes across in good time and then they make their presence felt. Venice is one such place, Glastonbury another, Culloden another. Places that make it possible to feel what *is*, out of the everywhere and into here, as George MacDonald put it. Another such place is the marble quarry on the island of Iona. That industrial intervention into the heart of a fairy hill has settled down to become a place of meditation. And if you wish, you can pick marble pebbles from the sea. Some sixty miles north, the Isle of Skye also has a marble quarry. It is in a sacred landscape. Close by is the ringing rock of Oscar from which one can keep an eye on the moon rising over the curved goddess hills of the Red Cuillin. Behind as one strikes the rock is the rough blue hill of Blaven, its name a seamless unity of Norse and Gaelic. Close also is a cave in which was found a trace of an ancient lyre. Was that instrument a gift from Orpheus to Ossian? Or did Orpheus merely lose it while trying to charm Cerberus? I would like that small object, the bridge of the oldest lyre, to have a museum devoted to it alone. A museum of the single thing. A museum of such modesty and yet of such moment that the best architects in the world would submit designs for it, and the significance of those designs would necessitate the building of a gallery to display them in some international art capital like Venice or Tokyo.

Reading my way towards Tennyson's *Akbar's Dream* I am absorbed in *The Death of Oenone*. The volume that contains both was the last book of the poet's work prepared in his lifetime. His art manifests there as a gathering of the past and a casting out towards the future. *The Death of Oenone* gathers the past as a narrative of dejection. The Trojan War is the background for Oenone's grief. Seamus Heaney explored an earlier phase of the story in his account of *The Cure at Troy*. The cure in question was that of the archer Philoctetes, whose arrows were destined to leave Paris mortally wounded. Paris would beg in vain for his wife, Oenone, to use her skills as a healer to save him. By contrast, in *Akbar's Dream* Tennyson casts forward from the new age he was helping to define in the 1890s to the new age of the 1960s where spiritual hope seemed to flutter for the West in the form of Zen and Sufism. I am struck again by the words of the sixteenth-century poet Abul Fazl: 'Sometimes I frequent the Christian cloister, and sometimes the mosque / But it is Thou whom I search for from temple to temple. / Thine elect have no dealings with heresy or orthodoxy / For neither of these stands behind the screen of thy truth. / Speculation to the heretic, theology to the orthodox, / But the dust of the rose petal belongs to the heart of the perfume-seller'. Tennyson uses those words to preface *Akbar's Dream.*

Ursula Le Guin writes that 'to be an atheist is to maintain God. His existence or his non-existence, it amounts to much the same, on the plane of proof'. Thinking thus, I found myself in prayer. I was in Inigo Jones's church of St Paul's in Covent Garden, a place that seems more than Christian. Turner's parents are buried there. So also is Robert Strange, the Jacobite engraver who survived Culloden. It is a place where one can meditate regardless of one's belief or lack of it. Few buildings made at the behest of religion actually foster prayer. Another that does so is Santa Sofia in Padua. It would seem from its name to have been built on an older site of goddess veneration. Ruskin did not pay much attention to it but he would have been interested in its carved capitals, some unfinished and yet complete in intention. The first time I visited that church I noticed a font. It had held the water with which Galileo's son had been christened in 1606. Four years later Galileo saw the moons of Jupiter for the first time. Inigo Jones would have appreciated the proportions of the Romanesque brickwork of Santa Sofia. I like to think he might have met Galileo during his sojourn in Italy.

It is a pity that Sir Christopher Wren's early conception of the other St Paul's was not accepted. It would have been a better, more centrally focussed religious building. Not a rival to Borobudur or

Angkor Wat but heading in the right direction. However, the plans were too radical for the English clerics of the seventeenth century and the bombast of the church that resulted has tended to keep me away from it, even from John Donne's memorial. It is curious to think that although I do not feel old or young or middle-aged I am, nevertheless, older than Donne was when he died. Have I done enough to be able to die? Had he? In my mind still are images of Angkor Wat, and Allen Ginsberg's words in praise of it. Will I ever go there? Should I? A temple is not so much a place of worship as a place around which the beauty and horror of life and death can flow, as they did so precisely in Cambodia, as they do so precisely in Syria as I write. Is a true temple ever ruined or destroyed? In some obvious sense the answer is yes: how can one deny it as yet another group of enthusiastic young men blow something apart somewhere in the service of some rationale or other? Yet a doubt remains. For a temple is not just a building but a place. Time flows around the temple. Life, of course. Death, if you will. In the temple, eternal, is love.

Yet all I can think of is snow. Yamagata. Glencoe. Perhaps it is the time of year I am writing. I remember driving into Glencoe going east on the A82 in a snowstorm. I was stopped at the mouth of the glen by road works, a red traffic light in the blizzard. The unseen presence of deer: Ossian's mother among them. A deer singled out in snow as in a painting by Courbet. A few hundred yards further along I stopped again to look up at a rock buttress that has Ossian's Cave at its heart. What was I? Pilgrim, tourist, passerby?

Alexandre Kojève writes: 'Nothingness nihilating as time in space [...] is what makes man a passerby in the spatial world'. Ian Hamilton Finlay had those words carved into a bench of slate in his garden. Close by is the hump of a milestone with on it the words: 'Man, a passerby'. When I first visited Finlay's garden of Little Sparta I asked the artist – or do I mean the poet? – if I could take some photographs. He asked me not to, because it was early in the year and 'nature was not yet ready'. On other visits nature was indeed ready, leaves screening Apollo in pursuit of Daphne, or Claude's signature in pursuit of balance. And the legibility of letters softening in old wood: 'Evening will come, they will sew the blue sail'. And again: 'Thesis/Fence; Antithesis/Gate; Synthesis/Stile'. A friend wrote of that one: 'Hegel made me laugh'. A passerby. Is that all any of us can ever be? Is the best that we can hope for some reverence in the moment of passing? What then in that moment can one revere? A sculpture? The glint of a river at twilight?

There are sculptures that I try to pass by when I can. Some are statues of writers, Robert Burns in Dundee or London, Balzac in Paris. Some have more universal spiritual intent. I used to make a point of visiting a colossal bronze Bodhisattva in the central courtyard of the Victoria and Albert Museum. But then the cherry trees around it were ripped up in a fit of redesign and the statue was moved. Later in that same city I found a head in stone of the archangel Michael, the work of Emily Young. Most temples named for Michael, like those named for Sophia, seem to link in a way more primordial than obvious. The burial place around the traces of an old chapel of Michael on the island of Little Bernera in the Outer Hebrides is one such place. It is above a beach of whitest sand where Gealachos, 'fair of foot' – she was the young priest's daughter – loved to walk. I value other Michael places like the Saxon church that is the true heart of Oxford. Will I retrace Henry Adams's tourist-pilgrim steps one day from Mont St Michel to Chartres? As I write, the unusual proximity of the moon to the earth tugs the tide over the causeway, making of Mont Saint-Michel a true island once again. Later, editing, and thinking of a book with Blake's *Glad Day* on its cover, I remember that Gael Turnbull writes of Lindisfarne: 'A hesitation of the tide / Betrays the island, daily'.

It is said that the name 'Michael' means 'who is like God'. So I thought to ask God: Who is like God? And God answered: 'I cannot tell you that, for like you I am a pilgrim'. A pilgrim: one who passes by with intent; a reverent traveller. Or one who becomes the path itself. The age into which I was born was an unusual period during which state-supported technological advance was, at least publicly, driven by a desire to explore rather than a desire to kill. I remember seeing the first images of the surface of the moon close up as a spacecraft orbited it. The sense of seeing those images came back to me in 2014 as I saw the view from another spacecraft: the stark beauty of the surface of a comet. As though I were a passer-by. A pilgrim: looking. The gesture of a lover that says: let me look at you as though I am seeing you for the first time. To travel is to look both outward and inward. To look and then to see is to echo the weave of light within oneself as a tree's branches echo its roots. An imperfect copy, like any echo or any weaving – for why would an artist want to copy perfectly? What would be the point? As a pilgrim or a writer I live to copy: not badly but differently.

Heraclitus's most irritating student noted that one cannot step into the same river even once. The original cannot claim to be a perfect version even of itself. The copy's claim to perfection lies in its imperfection. In as yet unburned libraries I honour those I have forgotten through the work of those who have reminded others of this and that by careful anthologising and editing. Who reads Robert Howard today? Yet: 'I attempt from Love's sickness to fly in vain, / Since I am myself my own fever and pain'. These refugee words from the past are new struck for every age.

As I write I read of a library burning in northern Iraq. The word becomes: what? Will fragments remain to inspire a new *Ossian*, a new *Werther*, a new

*Lover's Discourse*? We rebuild libraries as imperfect copies of ourselves, finding and treasuring scattered half-destroyed leaves of poetry from editions of Omar Khayyam or Robert Burns or Christina Rossetti. Why? Because that is what we do. 'The band is playing Auld Lang Syne / But the heart will not retreat'. Cannot retreat. Is a library always just an ember? A burned thing still warm from the joy of the iconoclast, and a glowing coal of thought and love for they who reimagine it, as looters come and go. Must a library sometimes be the most empty, most emptied, of things?

Once I was a designer of libraries, a puzzling yet rewarding quest. Martin Buber notes that one of the last great teachers of Hasidism is said to have addressed his pupils thus: 'I wanted to write a book called *Adam*, which would be about the whole man. But then I decided not to write it'. Wise.

Yet George MacDonald went ahead and wrote *Lilith*. So at least there is one title with which to start a library. Tennyson (or was it Whitman, or Ginsberg?) borrowed MacDonald's copy of Ossian's poems in Gaelic and Latin. It is easy to forget the libraries that were destroyed after Culloden. It is easy to forget that Macpherson's recreation of the lost epic of the north was demanded by his own history. Werner Spies called Macpherson's reinvention of the tales of his people 'a white lie'. An imperfect thing, the truth of which is in its imperfection.

Barthes is concerned with the imperfection of truth when he challenges us to draw a line that is not stupid. To meet that challenge, he notes that one must be *gauche*. One must make a gesture of pencil or pen that has a catch in it, a gesture that makes fragmentation inevitable. Drawing is itself thus an act of iconoclasm. Pencil and paper united in a love-death that neither would wish to survive. A graphic sacrifice and rebirth. Waddington writes that science's picture of the world is 'more like a portrait drawn by a painter than a precise theorem in logic'. We should not act as if we were surprised. In that imperfection is reality. When we copy, we are equally simple, equally imperfect. We must imitate Christ or Mithras or whomever, but nevertheless fail to be him. However imperfectly, we must still draw. The lover draws his lover's hair across her face in a gesture of truth. She thinks of him: 'His thunder is entangled in my hair / And with my beauty is his lightning quenched'.

A commentary to the *I Ching* notes that 'Life leads the thoughtful man on a path of many windings. / Now the course is checked, now it runs straight again. / Here winged thoughts may pour freely forth in words, / There the heavy burden of knowledge must be shut away in silence. / But when two people are at one in their inmost hearts, / They shatter even the strength of iron or of bronze. / And when two people understand each other in their inmost hearts, / Their words are sweet and strong, like the fragrance of orchids'. But sometimes one must wait. With the writer—it is attributed to Confucius—one knows that one's course is checked. That one must draw a line that is not stupid between what one says or writes or copies and what one does not. It is not easy. That line must be both itself and its boundary, its own keeper. A pilgrimage is that type of line. I am able to feel something of such a drawn way beneath and through my feet, whether through the chalk and flint of the Ridgeway or the granite and peat of the road to Smirisary. Or an old track, sometimes cobbled, through the mountain limestone landscape of northern Mallorca, the landscape of Ramon Llull and Robert Graves. It was on such a track that I glanced back and saw my shadow—or was it Pan? I think of those olive groves and I see in my mind's eye trees aflame in Palestine. Is such burning an act from which the soul of the iconoclast can ever recover?

A pilgrimage can be short. A few steps taken barefoot in frost becoming dew on grass in the early morning. Or just travelling. Looking out of the window of an aircraft and seeing a loved place, perhaps returning to it after a long absence—as Gaelic songwriters are prone to do—or seeing, with a shock of recognition, a place that one had only seen before in its image, as when I glanced down and saw the dark lava mass of Surtsey off the coast of Iceland for the first time. An essay by Donald Judd comes to mind: 'Some Aspects of Color in General and Red and Black in Particular'. In Iceland lava cools to a grey-black rock made porous by flaming vapour. Volcanoes create boulder sized jewels of black glass, facetted and beautiful, present yet absent, like a painted surface by Malevich, or slag glass from a destroyed steelworks. Now I read of a form of black made from carbon nanotubes, which absorbs so much light that the eye and the brain have virtually nothing to pick up on. An almost perfect copy of nothing. We can see it only in so far as we cannot see it. What if it were indeed a perfect copy of nothing? Would it coalesce with other thresholds of perception such as the speed of light where mass, it is said, becomes infinite, and absolute zero where all movement, it is said, ceases and surely matter must cease to be? Yet as an illusion? Once I saw three small paintings in a warehouse gallery above Tokyo Bay. Their dark surfaces were easy enough to make out: they nevertheless stood in for perfect copies of nothing. Yet they copied nothing. These works by Tomoharu Murakami occupied that space as fully as would have Mantegna's *Triumphs*, or a dense cycle of Byzantine mosaic.

If I were to describe black as an event, not a colour, I would call it nothing. If I were to describe red as an event, I would call it a fluctuation from nothing. A fluctuation that gives birth to time, that gives birth to light as a way of accounting for space. We can speak of a space as filled with light. If it were drained of light it would be in some sense empty, non-existent. A lack of being that is nevertheless able to become, to fluctuate into being. And that fluctuation is the breath that makes the black coal glow red. The lips are pursed in blowing as in a work by El Greco or La Tour. The *pneuma*. The word incarnate. Jean Ritchie sings 'Black is the colour of my true love's hair'. Mayakovsky reminds us that love is the heart of everything. The fluctuation from nothing.

Van Gogh's frustration was that he was unable to paint nothing. He had to make do with the physical world. But he shifted it and elided it, so that it became a little more like a performance of nothing. Art is the art of making noticeable. We notice, with Shakespeare, that the isle is full of noises. We notice, with Sesshū, that stones can be positioned in a garden. There is such a garden near Yamaguchi (in English: the mouth of the mountains). The rocks were drawn from the plateau of Akiyoshidai, renowned for the beauty of its limestone outcrops. Sesshū designed the garden towards the end of the fifteenth century. He lived on the other side of a ridge thick with bamboo forest. His house is sheltered enough, light enough, warm enough within which to produce a landscape scroll, or, if one were of a more Western inclination, the Book of Kells. But where the wonder of the achievement of the artist-monks of Iona lay in their ability to paint intricate detail, the wonder of the artist-monk Sesshū lay in his ability to refrain from doing so. To represent the void by itself. Neil Gunn writes of 'the uncanny feeling that these vague peaks were not simply apart in space but were being actively created by space. They were being born out of it. Space was the creative source'. When I first travelled to Sesshū's Yamaguchi, in the company of the artist Alan Johnston, I glanced out of the train and saw Mount Fuji as a void within a void, a sharp-edged softness of form cut from a deep haze made deeper by jetlag. Some time later, a station name gave me pause. Hiroshima. A modern-looking place, the home of many architects. One of them, Shinichi Ogawa, is a maker of buildings that tend to the void. Such was his house in the form of cube, made entirely of glass. A meaning rather than a residence. It was famous for a moment, but is now perfect only in its erasure. To which erasure the only response is a mark, a mark that is not stupid.

Sesshū understood that mark, as did Ruskin for a moment in his savage carelessness. So also did Hokusai when in old age he grasped simplicity and put aside colour to make *One Hundred Views of Mount Fuji* as his testament. Black is the colour of my true love's hair. 'Yet why the snow upon the raven tress?'

With Hafiz our song fluctuates from nothing and becomes time. Art is that fluctuation. A pencil line that is not stupid; a brushstroke of ink or paint. The dance of Shiva. Scientists like to reflect on that fluctuation. The Higgs particle, definitely—that is to say probably—found lurking in its high-energy lair on the border of Switzerland and France.

For Capra in *The Tao of Physics* the dance of Shiva is the energy of the Cosmos. For Coomaraswamy, it is the energy of humanity. There is no difference. How could there be?

Coomaraswamy began his career as a geologist; one of his earliest papers is about the marble of Iona and Tiree. A good training for an art historian, for an artwork like a book or a lump of rock is a material thing. A simple enough idea, as long as we remember that 'thing', at least in Iceland, means something like 'parliament'. A thing is a talking shop rather than an object. A nexus of energies. What could be a better description of matter? Except perhaps 'object', that is to say something thrown into opposition, exiled like lava from a volcano, or like a poet from a city or a court. One can think of matter as light in exile. And, of course, if matter is exiled it becomes light.

Le Guin writes of light as the left hand of darkness. Does that go far enough? Or must one also insist on the obvious, that darkness is the left hand of light? Yet as long as time exists in our minds light and dark cannot clasp each other, they are not in balance, however much we may wish it. They must run through history in a mutual chase, never quite reaching each other, like lovers only at one in their fate. Dante understood something of this. Paulo and Francesca, forever caught—as in Watts's painting—in a whirl of their own making. Or—as in Rodin's sculpture—in the beginnings of a kiss. The only question for us children of time is if that chase — which, for the want of a better expression, one might call *life* — is elegant or unedifying. That is the choice that myth offers. *La Vita Nuova*.

At last I came to the point of no return. Where was I, I wonder? Let us say I was at the top of a mountain, or in some sacred place, or having a cup of coffee, or talking to the cat, or seeing something in another person for the first time. There was no great fanfare to announce it but for a moment the void had opened and closed. I became a lover. 'And then we sever'. Time severs everything. It is the paradoxical gift with which we weave histories.

With time, Michelet created France and Tolstoy created Russia. Barthes writes engagingly of Michelet, but elsewhere he gives us an alternative in an image of twelve strokes of a Japanese brush that unite to mean 'nothing'. What is the difference? In *Ecclesiastes* I find both nothingness and time explored. Nearby in the text, Solomon and his lover sing of the detail of each other's bodies; and Wilfred Owen writes in his own *Song of Songs*: 'Even as Spring that laugheth into leaf; / Even as Love that laugheth after Life'.

As I write I become conscious that writing is not an elucidation of thought but an evasion of it. Yet the great evasion is not writing as such, but time itself. I evade, therefore I am. I evade nothing, and I have evaded nothing, therefore something is here. I exist in time and I accept that I must give up what I have every moment. 'And then we sever'.

That is the inconvenient message of the mistress of time and destruction, Kali. She fucks you and kills you and drinks your blood. There could be no better expression of the fact of time, that slight shift from nothing that gives identity. In my own life Kali was—courtesy of Joseph Campbell—the first deity to impress me. Later I discovered, to my surprise, the complementary nature as goddesses of sea and earth of Venus and Persephone.

Now I travel here and there, trying to distinguish sacred places from battlefields. A case in point: a well at Culloden. The Well of the Dead. Robert Burns wrote of those dead: 'Their winding-sheet the bluidy clay'. When Beethoven set those words, was he already writing his own ode to grief, his *Missa Solemnis*? To grieve is to grieve with all humanity. Yet to grieve is to be alone. 'And then we sever'. The fact of death sharpens the paradox. Is oblivion the consolation prize for those who accept nothing? I continue to evade thought, in the hope that my words may provide some kind of answer. I do not begrudge them their efforts to console me, but nor can I accept that they have been successful.

I cross the threshold. There is only one threshold. One might call it life, or love, but here I will call it death. In one type of Christianity that threshold is given form by what is called a 'lychgate', literally, in old English or Scots, a corpse gate. As in the *Lyke-wake Dirge* of the Scottish Borders. Such gates take the form of shelters, small temples marking the transition from secular to sacred, from thing to no-thing. An alternative such space is implied by the crossing of water. In the Highlands, corpses used to be carried through the landscape to a burial place. The route was along a path of truth, '*slighe na firinn*' in Gaelic, the term referring equally to the pilgrimage of the soul and of the body.

There is such a path that leads from Glen Finlas, where Millais painted Ruskin's portrait and flirted with Effie, over the high shoulder of Ben Ledi and down to the burial ground of St Bride by Loch Lubnaig. To reach that destination the River Leny must be crossed. Another such path leads through a pass between Glen Etive and Glencoe to a burial isle. The water is crossed; the gate opens and closes.

I have decided not to write a book called *Zen and the Art of Lychgate Construction*. Nevertheless, I cannot rid myself of the thought that it is at the lychgate that Buddhism is seamless with Christianity. Why do such structures look so Japanese? Is it because they are made to be no more than they need to be? What attracted modernist architects in Europe and America to Japanese aesthetics was the recognition of uncluttered functionality. But at the heart of that Japanese aesthetic is the acceptance of death, a point that can be missed in the western drive to everlasting life. The heart of life is death. They are one and the same. Perhaps the word 'love' can encompass both, as in 'God is love'.

As I write, my father approaches one such lychgate. He is dying. He has no choice in the matter; nor do I. I am reminded of Death playing chess with the knight in Bergman's *Seventh Seal.* Death plays a killer move against my father, one that has succeeded so often. Yet it fails and my father's evasion is admirable. But he is tiring. He taught me to play chess. Now death plays chess with him. It is a reminder to me to prepare myself for my own death. Not to accept it but at least to feel my way toward it. The effort in life as in death despite everything, must be to heed Barthes's exhortation to draw a line—or some equivalent—that is not stupid. The samurai artist and swordsman Musashi did that with every stroke of his brush and his sword. Was he mad or merely well balanced? I imagine Musashi standing in the shelter of a lychgate at Compton in the Surrey hills. Perhaps by the time that particular gate was built at the beginning of the twentieth century its Japanese appearance was actually influenced by Japan. It was made at around the time that Okakura was writing his *Book of Tea* to educate the West. What an education it still is: he writes of the Tea House as an abode of the Unsymmetrical dedicated to the worship of the Imperfect. Quite so.

At the same time, Charles Rennie Mackintosh, that master of imperfect symmetry, was attending to the East in the design of his art school library in Glasgow. That library—since fallen victim to the accidental iconoclasm of fire—was built when

Glasgow and its hinterland led the world in the aesthetics of the made thing, engineering, fine art, book design, it made no difference. Mackintosh was born into the age of the Clyde-built tea clippers, ships that have been a high point of maritime beauty ever since, among them Shakespeare's *Ariel* and Tennyson's *Sir Lancelot* and Burns's *Cutty Sark*, sailing technology designed to outclass the most advanced coal-and-steam-powered ships of the day. Such was the context for the development of Mackintosh's elegant modernism. Geddes wrote that 'the real artist is he who, like Mackintosh in the Art College of Glasgow [...] gets his effects within the sternest acceptances of modern conditions. For here never was concrete more concrete, steel more steely, and so on'.

I remember a reception at Tate Modern in London. Turning from the conversations in which I was not participating to look at the steel structure of the building, I saw in raised lettering on each girder the words 'Lanarkshire' and 'Scotland'. Geddes would have been intrigued by the cultural re-use of that turbine hall. He would have been less taken by the trashing of the working communities that had made possible its frame. In honour of such loss, one might exhibit there a skip full of rust, or fill the hall with the ash of industrial archives.

I used to paint. I still do. My paintings are often squares. Some of my paintings are finished. Others I have been painting for several decades. I would not describe them as abstract. In a sense each is a non-figurative self-portrait, or perhaps a portrait of the paint itself. If I had the skill I would like to make paint of ash or rust, or of a pigment that somehow implied both, as the colour of cooling lava implies both. Or a pigment as blood red as the wound in Christ's side. The legend of that wound is that it leads to the heart of that androgynous god; it takes the form of a vulva, as the medieval artists of Tintern Abbey understood so well. From my window, an hour before sunrise, I see Venus and Mars and Jupiter in conjunction. Venus seems almost within reach. Is that not always the way? Before my sight began to blur I remember dark Mediterranean nights enabling me to feel out the rule-straight line of the moons of Jupiter with the naked eye. A single photon may have been enough for me then. And the angled smudge of the Andromeda Nebula, clearer in peripheral vision. My mother, a practical and poetically minded woman, taught me about astronomy. She would have been at home in Hypatia's Alexandria. I wonder if I needed any education other than in the stars?

With Verdi, I imagine the Pleiades through Otello's eyes. They are setting in the dawn, as he and Desdemona embrace. An end and a beginning. *Vien... Venere splende!* Did Shakespeare really never see that radiant planet from the Venice that he was to imagine as Othello's home? If I were to indulge in the game of who really wrote Shakespeare's plays, I would suggest a Scot who survived a duel in Mantua in 1582 and cloaked himself in the identity of Will Shakespeare on returning to England. Later he would scribble: 'What's in a name? That which we call a rose / By any other name would smell as sweet'. Names are interesting things. Sometimes they can indeed be shrugged on or off like an old shirt, but often they are specific, as though branded into flesh. One must, perhaps, always deny or over-embellish such a name until one has some idea of its significance. The tale of Oedipus is about one such name. It depends on absence and puzzlement. 'Why is my name "swollen foot?" Was I born with swollen feet? They seem elegant enough now that I am a young prince of Corinth at the height of my physical powers. Although I admit there is a substantial scarring, as though I had been crucified at birth, or hung upside down in a tree with my feet stapled together; and sometimes some hidden memory scars my dreams'. Or something like that.

Thus we arrive at Freud's study. A framed print of Ingres's *Oedipus and the Sphinx* is to the right of the bookcase. Accessible at a glance. Freud came into being not so much to be read and believed, but to draw attention to the fact that we have, in general, neither looked nor read enough. For Freud, see Sophocles. For Sophocles, grasp the wider tale of the young man with the swollen feet. His destiny was to know himself at whatever cost, for in the end he found that he did not have the everyday luxury of denial. What happened was this: on a narrow road a chariot wheel bruised his foot. And from there things developed. Killing first. Then riddle solving. Then fucking. Then truth in all its inconvenience. But love? Perhaps that was Antigone's gift to him. Love, the great irony. The height and the depth.

The purpose of myth is education. Drawing out the height and the depth. It enables one to draw out one's meaning and lay it open to interpretation. Perhaps, like Oedipus, one desires to understand why one is called 'swollen foot'. Or perhaps one seeks to understand, like Daphne, in what sense one's feet must be rooted to the earth. The opposite of myth is what is sometimes called 'reality', but that is no more than convention. There is nothing wrong with convention; it is, after all, convenient, but it has no educational function. One cannot be educated into convention – one must be trained into it. Such training, like the training of a rose into a pergola, can be beautiful, necessary and wise, but it is not education. For, as Alasdair MacIntyre notes, an education – and in particular a philosophical education – must make one unfitted for contemporary society. What fits one for society but at the same time delimits society is training. From time to time, training becomes a mode of control with no other purpose than control.

Charlton Ogburn writes: 'We trained hard but it seemed that every time we were beginning to form up into teams we were reorganized. I was to learn later in life that we tend to meet any new situation by reorganizing, and what a wonderful method it can be for creating the illusion of progress while actually producing confusion, inefficiency, and demoralization'. Education does not create the illusion of progress. To progress, in the sense of to be educated, is – perhaps – to assert one's ownership of death. Such progress attracts metaphor. Dark woods, sea crossings, rivers, *et cetera*.

For me it was like this. When I was a good bit older than the thirty-five years that Dante claimed, I found myself in a dark wood that only I could see. Within that wood I waited without patience or hope. My path was not particularly difficult, but it seemed to have no meaning. Although I knew I had done certain things that had some moderate worth, it seemed to me that I was waiting for something that did not exist and what stood in for that non-existence was an awareness of death. Nevertheless, I had a sense of things returning, being reassessed and I found myself revisiting places not from nostalgia but rather to grasp something that had perhaps eluded me when I had been in that place before.

As I did so I found that I was a weaver of my own history, my intuition telling me such weaving must be done at the right moment, and that when there was no time to lose there was no time at all, only some sort of rhythm. I realised then that I lacked nothing, except my self, and a stone upon which to hone that self into being. I found that stone built into the wall of a church near Inverness. A sharpening stone. In Gaelic: *clach-gheurachaidh*.

Perhaps in life there is always a sharpening stone. For me it was a lover who shaped me as I had to be shaped. Had I not met her when I did, my life would have been formless. Had we not parted, I would not have seen that I was not yet myself. Time separates every being from eternity but it enables us to love, as though love were a stand-in for eternity, or as if time itself were love. Like the harmonics of a singing bowl—reverberation, all sound becoming light and all light becoming sound. Turner's later paintings have some such quality, some such implication. Such experience must echo to eternity in the heart or not at all. The Grail was sometimes said to be a woven thing, more a basket of willow than a bowl of gold. Perhaps there is no difference, for any chalice is an entanglement of energy, a thing woven in the mind of God, who is himself woven only by one's faith or lack of it. Now my father's death thuds into my life to hone me a little more. A surprising and total cosmic shock. A living being become briefly an effigy, his skin as beautiful as marble and then as beautiful as ash. I have no more to say, and yet I am only at the beginning.

I said farewell to my father in words marked by him in a poetry book that I discovered after his death: 'Flow down, cold rivulet, to the sea, / Thy tribute wave deliver: / No more by thee my steps shall be, / For ever and for ever. // Flow, softly flow, by lawn and lea, / A rivulet then a river: / No where by thee my steps shall be / For ever and for ever. // But here will sigh thine alder tree / And here thine aspen shiver; / And here by thee will hum the bee, / For ever and for ever. // A thousand suns will stream on thee, / A thousand moons will quiver; / But not by thee my steps shall be, / For ever and for ever'.

The more I read Tennyson, the more I know him to be a treader of the earth. There is a passage in *Idylls of the King* where Lancelot finds the Grail but realises it cannot be for him. Burne Jones shows Lancelot sunk in a dream with an angel of the Grail looking on. It is as close as he gets. So he returns to tread the earth again. For whom is the Grail? It is an unspeakable question yet that of which we cannot speak we must speak of anyway. There is only one river in my life, one moment, one day, one evening, one path trod. And it is gone now, yet ever present. For reality is loss and I am lost. Like Tennyson. That river poem is Tennyson at his most Blakean, easy to overlook in its simplicity.

I realise that I have done no more than create a reading and re-reading list for myself. A collection. I would like to think a library could be built to house it. Following Ruskin, I would want it to be fireproof, so that when – as would be inevitable once in while – scholars were killed or imprisoned and books were burned by the adherents of this or that new fashion in iconoclasm, at least the building would survive to be restocked. Any such restocking would, ideally, be made with books de-accessioned over the ages by other libraries. The material cultural history of each book would thus replenish the lost history of the library. With every replenishing a new version of history would be born and made vivid by belief in its objectivity.

The building itself would be the shape of a cube. It is a good architectural form that responds to the ordered and balanced separations needed in a library. A regular hexahedron, which one might find, for example, at the heart of an institute of education:

> I feel I must give some account here of my visit to the College of the Necessary Path (formerly known as the Chreodic College). Its four faculties are the traditional ones. The first, sited above the main campus in several field stations, is the Faculty of Mountain Gravity (which incorporates the schools of Epigenetic Landscape Studies and Ecological Physics). More centrally placed on the campus is the Faculty of Highland Space. Gunn-Sesshū contemplative methodologies are widely adopted here, although Stevensonian and even Humean views are also common. The dominant school is that of Waterfall Studies, but that is complemented by the School of the Carefully Placed Stone. Also based here is the Cloud Chamber project (Wilsonian). The third faculty occupies the well-resourced studio

complex, which makes such a visual impact as one clears the last hairpin bend on the approach to the college. This is the Faculty of Hand and Eye, which incorporates the School of Ecology of Mind. Close by is the cafeteria in its marvelous limestone cavern. Many of you will remember the views of the archipelago from there. The final stop on my visit was the Faculty of Stairs and Labyrinths. Deep within this faculty lies the hexahedral library that defines the knowledge handling of the college by specifying the relationships between different styles. Within that library one can see how the School of Empiricism depends on its co-schools of Rationalism, Classicism and Romanticism. My visit concluded with a reception on the terrace above the sea, followed by a sound sleep in the tented village.

True enough.

Japan comes to mind again. Was it there on the Inland Sea that the college was sited? Or was it on the coast of Somerset looking towards Wales? Or could it have been in Ramon Llull's Mallorca? Or tucked away in some corner of Cape Breton? Were it not for the limestone geology so evident in the cafeteria, Iceland would have been high on the list. My search for the college has been long and difficult. Time and time again it has seemed to be within my grasp but then like Lancelot in the proximity of the Grail, I have lapsed into a deep dream. There is no way of waking from such a dream (which is sometimes known as reality) but one can help oneself to recognise its nature. Museums exist to foster that process of recognition. What other purpose could they possibly have? If I were to form a new museum I would begin by plundering older collections, in sympathy with their original acquisition policies. From the British Museum I would acquire a head of Hercules, a small reproduction of the Laocoon, and a nearby bust of Minerva; and possibly a Minoan Sphinx lintel. From the Pitt Rivers I would take nothing, although I would attempt to acquire the museum's soul. Were that possible, a whole hall would be devoted to it. Another area would be devoted to forgeries that were noticeably better than their originals. A mezzanine floor would be reserved for the finest Japanese vending machines. Leading off it would be a comfortable cloister where the visitor could relax and consume tubs of green-tea ice cream.

Yet as I write this I can feel the form of the proposed museum beginning to lack focus, and I feel that I must abandon the project and return to the desert, like a saint painted by Bellini. Perhaps it is only in the desert that anything becomes possible.

'The desert were a paradise, if thou wert there'. I remember the first time I saw a reproduction of *Dante and Beatrice* by Henry Holiday. Do I engage now with Dante's thought or do I just re-engage with that moment of childhood pleasure? In any case I find myself turning to Petrarch, to Neruda, to Borges, and I mix their words into a surreal pudding of love and lust and memory, yet I am unsatisfied. So I bathe myself in the verse of Hafiz and hope for the best. Thus hoping, I find myself on the seashore with Tagore (and perhaps with Odysseus) and with Sorley MacLean. For Sorley might have written, were he Hafiz, 'And when, with soul and body burned, I fell / Dust at her feet—she gave me to the wind'. And Hafiz might have written, had he been MacLean, 'And if I were on the shore of Moidart / with you, for whom my care is new, / I would put up in a synthesis of love for you / the ocean and the sand, drop and grain'.

It all leaves me more or less confused. One of the stranger aspects of living through an extent of life (the phrase 'getting older' does not quite seem to catch it) is that understanding becomes less accessible *via* words, yet at the same time one needs to have at least read and perhaps understood a vast heap of words in order to approach that inaccessible thing or nothing that seems to be of interest. Strangest of all is that those words which remain most useable tend to be very old formulations of this and that (or I and Thou) and teeter themselves on the edge of the non-verbal. The *I Ching* is notable in this regard. An old text, and at the same time a drawing of changes. But also in one of its methods a dance of the hands, manipulating yarrow stalks to evoke number and thence the simplest of structures, a line. Each line solid, or open like the earth itself quaking open as Hades emerges to abduct Persephone; then closed and bright with gathered flowers.

Of all the three rather unconvincing big boy Greek gods, Hades is the least impressive. A non-entity, saved from erasure only by the goddess who deigned to complete him. It does not matter if we call her Persephone or Demeter, they are one and the same. They needed a man and Hades was convenient. I suppose if one were to rethink Hades in a more positive light he would be a deity of earth, a Green Man. Persephone would garland him as Guinevere might Lancelot, or as Europa did the bull on the shore.

'I would put up in a synthesis of love for you / the ocean and the sand, drop and grain'. The poet claimed those words as only an echo in English of his original Gaelic. Can one understand the progression of the years without such love? As we draw or fail to draw our gauche lines, our lines that are or are not stupid? I write as though I had thought about such things but I have not. Not yet. To write is simply to put off thought, to put off the unwritten next sentence. As to live is to push death into the future, again and again. Once I had a lover. There is so little in that sentence, and yet it is full to the brim. It is the pot that spills over to show the universe, the Grail that Lancelot is unable in the end to accept. His sea journey, as Tennyson recounts it, did not—it seems – imply readiness, but at least it was a journey. A journey of the heart, and yet the heart may not be evident until death. What will be understood then of each of us? A few verses marked in an anthology. Or five or six curious seashells found in a pirate's sea chest. 'It has often set me thinking since' writes Stevenson (in the person of Jim Hawkins) 'that he should have carried about these shells with him in his wandering, guilty and hunted life'.

In *El Hacedor*, Borges writes of another journey, the journey into blindness. He writes in the person of Homer: 'Why did these memories keep coming back to him, coming back like a simple prefiguration of the present?'. The past is after all the same country, the same entangled instant. Wittgenstein comments: 'I read: "philosophers are no nearer to the meaning of 'Reality' than Plato got". What a strange situation'. For Plato, read Homer. Why should jealous rage still be such an enchanting prospect? Yet it seems to get at something, as a pirate's collection of seashells gets at something. Something that one might notice and come to terms with. Is it too simple to say that the human condition is to rage and to collect things? Then to either notice what one is doing, or not? A great deal of myth is about noticing before it is too late, or noticing and it being too late anyway. 'Know thyself' is the injunction of any oracle. It is good advice. Eve's knowledge enabled Adam to begin that process of knowing himself. His first knowledge was that he had been ignorant of the fact that he and Eve were naked, and thus the fashion industry was born. The earliest garment was, apparently, a fig leaf, a strangely difficult thing to wear but the leaf of one of the most symbolic of all fruits. A fruit that welcomes and rewards the loving caress of a mouth. So: not an accidentally chosen leaf. A leaf worthy of *L'Origine du monde*.

In Paris in 1929 Man Ray pushed Courbet's boundaries further and brought images of fucking within the purview of the modern artist. Ruskin would not have been amused but Queen Victoria, an altogether more sexual being, might have been. Man Ray scratched at the hypocrisy of his time and ours, so much so that these works tend to be glossed over in the literature about him and are little reproduced. The guidebook for our late-Ruskinian cultural uneasiness, Freud's *Das Unbehagen in der Kultur* was published that same year of 1929, as economies crashed and politicians took the opportunity to become more strident. Ten years later, both Freud and Man Ray had fled mainland Europe in the face of anti-Semitism, Freud to London, Man Ray to Hollywood. Sometimes what passes for religious persecution is in fact the oppression of cultures whose members are, for one reason or another, able to think freely. Jewish culture — the culture contained by that Venetian invention, the Ghetto — was throughout much of European history one such culture. It is interesting to think that the

Ghetto was a place in which freedom of thought was imprisoned but only at night. Was it too dangerous to allow such thinking to wander in the hours of darkness lest it become one with the dreams and lovemaking of the other citizens of Venice?

The poet has no freedom other than to repeat, so I retranslate Osip Mandelstam, casting prose poetry from English versions of his Russian stanzas:

> I had not heard blind Ossian's tales, I had not tasted that old wine, so why do I find myself in my imagination in a forest clearing? Why do I think as I look up that I see Scotland's blood-red moon? I hear the rooks cawing and the sound of the harp reflected into ominous silence. And I see in my mind's eye warriors' tartan fluttering in the breeze, warriors' shields flashing in the moonlight! But in contrast to this wonderful rambling dream with which my fellow poet has deluged me, the neighborhood looks dull indeed. That's the thing about poetry: it jumps generations until suddenly some bard like me composes it again as his own.

Are my words any nearer to their inspiration than Werther's aria is to Macpherson's Berrathon? Could they, in any sense, be closer? As a lover cannot be any closer to the beloved? The relationship of lover and beloved is that of music. Beethoven's string quartet Opus 130 culminates in a great fugue. That fugue is implied in the first note of the first movement. It is one of the ironies of musical history that Beethoven was persuaded to write another conclusion to the work because of the challenge of that fugue. If performers are tiring and unable to give it the intensity it requires, what of it? The same is true of singers of Isolde by the time they get to the *Liebestod*. That is the point: at that point one must sing or play as if exhaustion and death did not matter. For they do not.

The story of the Irishwoman Iseult and the Cornishman Tristram. One version is as follows: The hero Tristram fought and nearly died, a splinter of Q-Celtic blade deep in his side. Iseult the healer began to bring him back from death, finding that sharp shard of iron and tugging it out and in the process wounding herself, her blood finding that of Tristram as if it were her own. With that it began and neither knew what was to come, Iseult least of all, as she mourned and buried and swore to avenge her beloved brother, killed by the deceptive thrust of some uncouth foreigner. Afterwards she touched her brother's sword, cutting her finger on its broken edge, shocked to find the echo of that shard she had found edging Tristram's heart, and her mind jarred and shattered as she weighed Tristram's life against her own history. But she stayed her hand, sensing that this was just the first unravelling and ravelling of all that she and he could and must ever be. Then in that confused clarity the hero woke to laughter and beauty and loved Iseult his foe and his saviour and despite herself and despite him she already loved him as herself but not herself. And time ran on ahead again inexorable as Iseult felt the hardest accuracy of despair for she knew that what little wisdom Tristram had was young and light—as the wisdom of men so often is—and that in his duty-bound manner he would think it right to sacrifice his love for the good of a mere kingdom. The fool the fool, the audience shouts out as if attending at a pantomime. You fool you fool you fool—and yet without Tristram's quaint naivety there would be no plot no life no death, no Iseult as she transcends every space every time every thing and every one as finally she stands alone singing for the multitude honouring the death of Tristram her lover her friend her fate her guest.

The news comes through that Umberto Eco is dead. In 1977 he published a guide for his students; the first English-language version was published in 2015 as *How to Write a Thesis*. It is a book passionate in its distaste for the un-thought-through. Despite the information revolution between times, most things that matter to Eco remain the same. An actual difference is that the book emerges from the age of the typewriter. Images of some of Eco's typewritten index cards are reproduced in the English language version to illustrate his method. Or rather they seem to be reproduced. In fact they are emulations: rivals, translated yet presented as if they were not. Vying for an impossible identity of indiscernibility. Schopenhauer writes that 'only by ordering what one knows by comparing every truth with every other truth can one take complete possession of one's knowledge'. In *The Name of the Rose*, Eco writes of books murmuring to one another about their truths. *How to Write a Thesis* is about how one might tap into that murmuring and express one's insight in an ordered manner. A resonance comes through a friend, a scholar of Chinese, who recommends a recently published version of the *I Ching*. The use of Latin here and there intrigues me. I find that these tags derive from Jesuit interpretations of the text in the early eighteenth century. The translator illuminates these by association with the utterances of the heretical vagabond Salvatore in *The Name of the Rose*. The Latin deepens my experience of the text, historicising it and adding another rhythm.

Inevitably I find myself flipping through Helen Waddell's *Mediaeval Latin Lyrics* (this particular copy a battered duplicate de-accessioned by the National Library of Scotland). One of the poems she collects, *Ms of Monte Cassino*, gave its title to a sculpture by Eduardo Paolozzi. It can be found at the top of Leith Walk in Edinburgh. The work is centred on a dismembered foot which is resonant not only with the wartime destruction of the monastery of Monte Cassino but with the psychological fragmentation of Paolozzi's own wartime experience: interned as an Italian Scot, then drafted into the Pioneer Corps, and at last escaping to art school (where else?). His sculptural comment is personal and mythological, making reference to his ancestral home, self-portraits, and the lame artificer Hephaestus. The foot is a massive lump of bronze. I am partial to such sculptural lumps. Another such is the Belvedere Torso. A great big block of stuff. In my experience it occupies a stairwell as only Hercules could. I have never seen the original or the copy—if it is such—that is thought of as the original.

My experience is of a battered plaster cast in an art school in a northern European city. I feel myself in its muscle-bound stoicism as though I were myself a block of marble. Donne writes: 'That which in him was faire and delicate, / Was just the milke, which in love's childish state / Did nurse it: who now is growne strong enough / To feed on that, which to disus'd tasts seems tough'. For the moment at least the words seem to refer to Hercules, his labours. For he had to understand himself as a mortal being, feed himself on the tough meat of life. Like Christ; like anyone. Looking at the torso again, I feel it as a block not of carved marble or cast plaster but of poured concrete with an armature of tough but rusty reinforcement bars protruding, dumped by some local upheaval into the shallows of time. Where I find it.

A bit later I find an echo from Felicia Hemans: 'And thou, triumphant Wreck; e'en yet sublime / Disputed trophy claimed by Art and Time'. She is referring to Napoleon's looting of the sculpture from the Vatican.

Another guide to method from that year of 1977: my copy of C. H. Waddington's *Tools for Thought* once belonged to the library of Oxford Polytechnic and was de-accessioned when the college was rebranded as a university. Colleges with 'technic' in their titles were erased from history during the same period that the British economy plunged from the solidity of manufacturing into the false wealth of deregulated credit. The word became discarnate and the hand and eye skills – trade skills – that Einstein advocated for every thinker were lost. *Tools for Thought* is a book about how systems develop along necessary paths. It is also about how systems can collapse catastrophically. Catastrophe as necessity. Did Oedipus tread the most necessarily catastrophic path of all to a point where three roads met? A choice seemed to be offered to him, but it was not. Did he cope well with his fate? Do I cope well with mine?

Ruskin's fate was to be Turner's great advocate while failing to understand his work. As when he tells us with great authority all about the technical failings of Turner's painting *The Golden Bough*. Yet, however wrong he is, he makes us look at it. In his usual manner, he goes up close, ignores what distresses him about the work as a whole, and falls in love with the detail, and makes the detail speak for the whole. I too look at that detail. In the grand sweep of Turner's achievement it can be missed.

I find myself again in Ruskin's debt, if no more inclined than usual to agree with him.

In a charity shop in Somerset I find Helen Waddell's *Lyrics from the Chinese*. Later I discover that it is her first book, published originally in 1913. The edition in my hand dates from 1921: 'The morning glory climbs above my head, / Pale flowers of white and purple, blue and red. / I am disquieted'. The original was written about three thousand years ago. Did a scholar of that time also write a book about thesis writing? If we could read such a work today would anything have changed? It would be convenient to think we can do some things better now. Perhaps we can, here and there. We can make wonderful things like firth-spanning bridges, computers, spacecraft, *et cetera*. And we still write poetry and bind books. But we do not seem to be able to lead. Are we less good at that? We do not seem to want to avoid war enough. We avoid declaring war, as if it were unseemly to do so. But the real unseemliness lies in the continuous nature of our undeclared wars.

Bodies politic in the end must perform their own deaths. The only question is how many souls they will take with them this time around. Once in a while an Akbar or a Mandela or a Martin Luther King emerges to give us hope that there is a way to govern other than by killing. But that soon passes. The bombing starts again in Baghdad or Brussels or Cambodia or Gaza or London or Istanbul or Dresden. The smart money is invested in the arms industry. And Walter Benjamin wanders the arcades of Paris wanting to buy that elusive first edition of Kafka, but knowing he should flee. He is too late. Is it always too late?

The market for stolen artefacts thrives. Art theft is a kind of asymmetrical iconoclasm. The work disappears as if destroyed; then it re-appears as if by magic somewhere else, glossy with money and praise, any inconvenient history or blood wiped away. There is a book called *The Gods are Leaving the Country*. It is not about atheism: it is about the stealing of art. The country in question is Nepal. Despite all of that the art survives to allow those who experience it to explore the secrets of their own hearts. I find a book about the old kingdom of Angkor. I am aware as I look at the images that I may be looking at things no longer there.

I find an image on the Internet. A face half chiselled off by a looter. Not long ago. How many more are gone? How many such fragments now grace apartments in Berlin or Melbourne or Vancouver, their damaged states adding a frisson of uncertainty to their perceived authenticity? Does that matter? Does it matter that bronzes by Rodin were melted when the World Trade Center was destroyed? Does it matter that along with drones and tanks the destruction of those New York skyscrapers now forms the subject matter of Afghan rugs? Does it matter that the Buddhas of Bamiyan no longer exist? It is fruitless to expect answers. On the positive side one can note that iconoclasm makes one think about art.

From my father I inherit a pair of binoculars and a pair of magnifying spectacles. They are tools for exploring macrocosm and microcosm. The Andromeda Nebula or an engraved line. Yet I feel that I lack insight. Oedipus blinded himself on discovering the truth; I hope I can avoid the need for such drastic action. I cannot remember exactly why Tiresias became blind but it was some kind of fate-mandated balance. I think it was deemed enough by the gods that he had known the pleasure of lovemaking from the points of view of both man and woman.

Eco's death has jogged me to re-read this and that. In the end I settle for *Reflections on the Name of the Rose*. I think I prefer the American title: *Postscript to the Name of the Rose.* 'Reflections' seems a little too involved, a little too comprehensive, a little too explanatory. Because of Eco's typewritten index cards I find myself looking for photographs of typewriters. One is from the Scottish Poetry Library and it shows the machine used by Edwin Morgan. Another, dating from 1928, is by the Italian/Mexican photographer Tina Modotti. It is the typewriter of her lover, Julio Antonio Mella. The next year Mella was shot while walking with Modotti. Her image of his typewriter remains. As do her images of his face, beautiful both in life and in death. I have always respected the work of another of her lovers, Edward

Weston. A dead pelican, a steelworks, his images of Modotti herself. Neruda wrote of her 'fragile life' after her death in 1942, a death as unresolved as that of Mella. In 1973 Neruda himself died in a way as yet unresolved. Searching the Internet I find an image of his typewriter.

The strike of a manual typewriter gives rise to a letter on a sheet of paper. Sometimes the writer's finger slips and the letter becomes a shadow of what it might have been. A poem written in this way has a reality of almost permanence, a reality of loss. I imagine Neruda writing his *Veinte poemas de amor y una canción desesperada* in such a manner. A friend sends me some references to Tanizaki's *In Praise of Shadows*. Does Tanizaki say anything about the shadowy nature of typewriting? Where is my typewriter? Did I give it away? There is something convincingly causal about those simple well-designed machines. I can find no image of Eco's typewriter. For now, I think of it as a sort of dream able to create the impression of letters from nothing. I think of meaning impressed on a page by a combination of typewriter key-strikes as a fluctuation from nothing much like the birth of the universe. The former a semantic translation *ex nihilo* as the latter is a temporal translation *ex nihilo*. The logos of nothing translated into the pneuma of something. To think is to breathe. The materiality of thought, the physicality of meaning. Nothing as substance, as understanding: that which stands below while we ponder, steadying ourselves on the fact of a doorframe.

Sesshū strove for an identity in indiscernibility of something and nothing in every brushstroke made or withheld. Titian's quest was much the same when he painted his last canvases with his fingers. Through gesture both artists became their work. In one of those works Titian adds a layer by showing himself as a kingly judge who is unwise enough to tell the truth and by doing so accidentally condemns a fellow mortal to death. As Marsyas is flayed the word becomes discarnate. *En route* to his death Marsyas is proud and eager to please. But then he is tortured into an understanding of his mortality. *The Dream of the Rood* without the young hero. Titian seems, on the face of it, to use his art to explore every nuance of life and myth, sensual or intellectual. But even he could not paint the cosmic unity that is the cunt. A few years before his *Flaying of Marsyas* he had shown the goddess Diana introducing a hunter to the hounds of his own desire. A clothed man discovers the naked goddess bathing with her retinue of nymphs. A crouching nymph in that painting was for Kenneth Clark one of the most seductive nudes in all art. Yet, goddess or nymph, they are all in the end non-sexed, their genitals denied in the traditional classical manner. Ruskin would have been happy enough as he stalked the fireproof, fuckproof, gallery of his imagination. Between Titian's *Diana and Actaeon*, finished in about 1559, and Courbet's *L'Origine du monde* of 1866 there are occasional serious efforts to do something about this denial, for example, the images of the architect Jean-Jacques Lequeu. He was thirty-two at the time of the French Revolution and was in his own way a visual revolutionary. His drawings of anatomy, while structurally intriguing, are limited by a commitment to reason rather than emotion, but it is clear that he reveres his subject matter. He draws architectural volutes (or French Revolutionary ringlets) of pubic hair. His work is a reminder that even after Courbet's efforts three quarters of a century later there was little acknowledgment of that hirsute beauty in painting until Valadon's image of herself as Eve in 1909.

The next year the young Imogen Cunningham eased away from the self-censorship of the fine art photography of the day and asserted the future of the medium with a simple picture of a family bathing in a river. There is a photograph by Judy Dater taken some six decades later. It shows the elderly Cunningham working with one of her models, still exploring the interplay of human and photographic form, still photographing outdoors. Cunningham's 1910 images look forward to a photography less fettered by Ruskin's doubts about flesh. At the same time her early work leads one back—*via* Annan and Stieglitz and Steichen—to see again that most Victorian of painters, G. F. Watts. The debt to Watts is surprising but substantial and it enables one to appreciate his confrontation with love and death as a way out of the Victorian moral straightjacket as well as being a defining quality of it. The Victorians had to confront death honestly. Death was close to them at all stages of life and across all classes. It did not confuse them as it does us as we extend our lives with this or that medical breakthrough as though remaining alive had some sort of intrinsic importance. With that in mind I let Tennyson lead me into the jaws of death. Where else? *Es la hora de partir. Oh abandonado!*

I imagine cities with names like 'Buenos Aires' where blind librarians lean on every marble pillar and Callas's voice drifts from every café radio. And tanks warm up their engines in this and that barracks, as they do also eternally in Glasgow and in Prague and in Santiago and in Beijing. I note the seduction of weaponry. *Et in Arcadia Ego* in the hands of Ian Hamilton Finlay: nature over again after Poussin with the help of military hardware. Paul Nash or Eric Ravilious could have shown us this. What Nash shows me instead in watercolour and photograph are standing stones at Avebury; what Ravilious shows me is chalk downland. Almost out of sight, a glimpse of a horse engraved on a hill, near the spot where the Green Man – some call him St George – confronted the dragon, under the gaze of a woman.

In *The Art of War* Sun Tzu writes: 'This is all / A matter of / Forms and / Dispositions'. Ryokan writes: 'Lying in my freezing hut, unable to sleep; /

only the quiet roar / Of water pouring over a cliff'. Is there a difference? One must presume so. For Sun Tzu time is subordinated to space, for Ryokan space is subordinated to time. 'The torrent pours down the rock / No hut receives me from the rain / Forlorn on the hill of winds'. Ryokan was born in 1758. At the age of almost seventy he fell in love. He lived out his final days with Teishin, a woman forty years his junior. Were it not for her we might not have his work. 'Our lives are like the plants / floating along the water's edge / illumined by the moon'. A matter of forms and dispositions.

Sun Tzu speaks of terrain: accessible, entangling, deadlock, enclosed, precipitous, distant. If, like Narcissus, you were to stop and look at your reflection in a deep pool, what began as a walk with your lover might end with your lover as nothing but a reverberation in the air. Such are the regulations of fate. The grit that gives discomfort and grip. The grit that gives deliverance. A shard of carved marble shattered by war. Will some talented conservator be able to reconstruct the ruins of Palmyra—which were already ruins when they were explored for Western archaeology in the eighteenth century? Yet does even the memory of such ruins matter? Evidently it does, to me at least. There is a Buddhist practice in which all that is made is unmade and that which has been unmade is given to the sea. It is the making and unmaking of a mandala of sand. When the mandala is unmade the sand is swept with care and great attention into bags. The sand is then distributed from those bags, some of it to those present at the act of deconstruction but most conveyed with due ceremony to a river or to the ocean so that those sacred grains can in time encircle the globe.

My arms disintegrate as I attempt to embrace clouds. So Baudelaire tells it, so Paolozzi shows it. Yukio Mishima writes: 'Do I, then, belong to the heavens?'. As Icarus I plunge into the ocean: Bruegel captures that bit. A tiny detail of his painting makes the point. Another who plunged into the ocean was Hephaestus, terrifying in his newborn ugliness. The lame god who became the lover of Aphrodite. Love is worthy of thought. It tempers one. The ancient Greeks understood that a single notion could not capture it. So they opted for four. And should one have been able to truly feel all of those loves, then perhaps one had lived, or become God, or died, or some such thing. To plunge into water is to be tempered—and every thought must be tempered. *Temperare*: to mingle, to restrain. Baptism is an act of tempering. I am mingled with and restrained by thee, for your love tempers me. For Icarus did such tempering come too late? Or was striking the water like a blunt blade just the beginning for him? To be truly tempered may require more than one lifetime. At Edzell there is a stone relief showing the figure of Temperance, uniting water and wine in dynamic balance. It is to be found in something of a Grail garden that allows one to proceed and vacillate—much as one would meditate with the trumps of a Tarot pack—to a doorway the purpose of which I do not know. Above it a female figure holds a chalice. She is the figure of faith. She does not lead nor does she offer. Nevertheless, something is implied.

I do not understand the tempering of sword blades but there is an intriguing difference between the focussed folded solidity of Japanese blades and the flexibility of Chinese blades. The swords of Kurosawa on the one hand and of Ang Lee on the other. Ang Lee's *Crouching Tiger, Hidden Dragon* is a tempering of one thing with another. He comments:

> My team and I chose the most populist, if not popular, genre in film history—the Hong Kong martial arts film—to tell our story, and we used this pop genre almost as a kind of a research instrument to explore the legacy of classical Chinese culture. We embraced the most mass of all art forms and mixed it with the highest—the secret martial arts as passed down over time in the great Taoist schools of training and of thought.

Such interrogative thinking is at the heart of what one might want to call, for want of a better word, 'art'. Art is the act of questioning. The conviction of the artist is that the question is in itself worth asking even if it cannot be answered, even if it cannot even be formulated. Thus art offers context. Shakespeare's art lies in the prelude, the context you hardly remember: 'She should have died hereafter—there would have been a time for such a word'. Tomorrow and tomorrow: the fugue. Prelude past and future fugue tempered by one another. And the present is—what? A way of seeming to intervene in some meaningful way: the finger on the keyboard of the piano or computer. There is no room for cleverness in the present, only some kind of return. But return to what? To the way—as Taoism would suggest? For Ruskin, the return was always to a truth, perhaps genuine enough but yoked to an irrelevant morality. Poor man. Or am I again speaking of myself? For Barthes, the return must be to the line that is not stupid. Would that include the key-strike of a typewriter?

In Kurosawa's *Throne of Blood* arrow after arrow after arrow strikes Macbeth. He is in the company of death. A hail of bullets for the revolutionary or the tyrant; a vision of angels for the pious; for the classicist, an encounter with Cerberus. There is a graveyard at Boleskine by Loch Ness. After Culloden an altercation broke out between a funeral party and a passing troop of Redcoats. The pits left by musket balls on tombstones tell a story that does not seem to have been fully written. Every mark is a reminder of what is the case. Everyone dies. That is clear enough. I die therefore I am. Dying is the absolute proof of my existence. It answers a question. The point is in the deposition (perhaps in Rubens's sketch in the Courtauld Institute), the pietà (perhaps in one of Michelangelo's rougher works in Florence), the entombment (perhaps as copied by Etty from Titian). Not in the crucifixion (although if crucifixion were the point, it would be represented here by Grunewald's work) or the resurrection (although if resurrection were the point it would be represented by Piero). Christ gave us the gift of eternal death should we wish to accept it. Yet the rood endures in every orchard. The tree of life from which the goddess Eve plucked the apple.

I can't quite get hold of my meaning. Perhaps my words should contract, hold themselves within themselves to preserve their existence. Like the compact muscled body of a Greek hero. Achilles's newborn muscular heat was quenched in the dark mirror of the Styx to make him almost immortal. A tempered weapon designed to lay Troy to waste. Does that help me to understand? Does it help to remember a lover who quenched and tempered me, making me useful for a moment? Do artists paint self-portraits because the act of looking in the mirror is itself an act of tempering, a quenching of the self within the self? Did Narcissus take it just a little too far? Or not far enough? Psyche sought her reflection in Cupid but at first found only darkness, invisibility. Perhaps love should not be revealed. One should not be quenched and tempered but kept in ignorance. Like Ruskin. Heroic in failure but a lover in his own mind nevertheless.

A pocket edition of Ossian, carefully rebound. A faint pencil note refers to Blake's *Visions of the Daughters of Albion*. Macpherson's heroine Oithona becomes Blake's Oothoon and I am tempered by Blake's sense of violence and tenderness. Will the proximity of his text enable me to write a line that is not stupid? 'Blake was *gauche*'. Is that sufficient? It would be better typed out on an index card, its materiality insisted upon. A figure from Michelangelo inspired Blake's engraving of Joseph of Arimathea, Joseph the metallurgist whose feet trod the turf of Glastonbury. Some say his nephew was at his side, learning about things. And then all hope was gone until Arthur came, and legend became true in the usual manner. In Blake's vision, 'she who burns with youth and knows no fixèd lot; Is bound / In spell of law to one she loathes'. Oothoon is bound to her rapist and her true lover is bound to his theocracy. Rape as iconoclasm. The breaking of the image that must be remade. In Macpherson's vision, the raped Oithona dies in battle against her oppressor as Yazidi women of today die in battle. After Culloden, Highland Rape. Macpherson understood that. It took a fashion designer working over two hundred years later to state it in that concise way, rethinking it for us. The Highlander Macpherson is buried in Westminster Abbey. The Londoner McQueen is buried in Skye. In their several ways both understood the geography of cultural paradox. It is fitting that the fabric banned for much of Macpherson's life became a key component of McQueen's tailoring brilliance.

Eco's index cards prompt me to acquire an Imperial Good Companion typewriter dating from the 1950s. It has an uncluttered cold-war aesthetic. As more ex-library books arrive in varying conditions I think about becoming a bookbinder. When was the first book sewn in signatures? Even an ex-library book can turn up 'unopened', its signatures un-cut, much of the text inaccessible. There was a time when I tried to avoid the questions that I had to ask. As though I were myself a densely written but inaccessible text, the signatures of my heart unopened. Perhaps it would have been safer if I had left them that way. Instead, like Ruskin, I find myself heroic in failure, but a lover nevertheless.

I read on the Internet that scientific research on palm trees in the Central Australian Desert finds itself echoing Aboriginal legend. The information was communicated by tradition bearers for a minimum of seven thousand years, perhaps much longer. A tough cultural subtext to the disagreement between James Macpherson and Samuel Johnson was the validity or otherwise of oral tradition. Johnson was invested in the magic of the written word, physical yet discarnate. The word cut loose from voice and memory, and nestled safely in a dictionary, like a flea. In the beginning was the word that was written and lost forever on the page. There are anthropologists who speak of arts that begin with the voice and arts that begin with the hand. Can that give a clue, in Ariadne's sense of a ball of thread to guide thinking? Her hand-spun thread enabled Theseus to return from the heart of the Labyrinth. Yet Theseus should not have required it to find his way, for a labyrinth is a singular path that twists and turns but on which one cannot get lost. That is as clear at Knossos as it is in the labyrinth of pilgrimage at Chartres. The significance of the thread is that of connection, direction, ethos, return. It gave Theseus the authority to conquer the monster of his fear. Does the written word confer that kind of authority on the reader and the writer, threading them together through the page? This essay is a kind of a threading. And I find that I have paused, offering myself the possibility of conclusion.

Finis

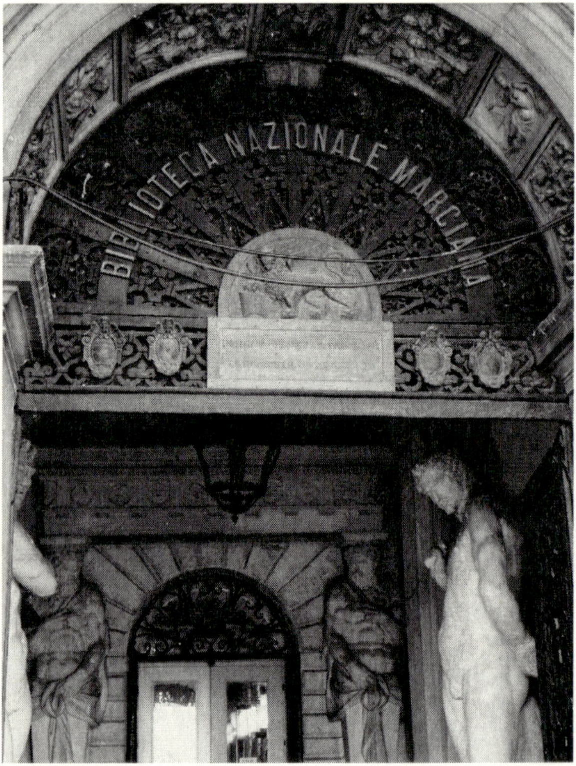
BIBLIOTECA NAZIONALE MARCIANA

BY WAY OF ACKNOWLEDGEMENT

# A LIBRARY


ADAMS, Henry, *Mont Saint Michel and Chartres*, Boston: Houghton Mifflin, 1913

AGEE, Chris (ed.), *The Other Tongues*, Belfast: The Irish Review, 2013

ANDERSON, J. R. L., & Fay Godwin, *The Oldest Road: An Exploration of the Ridgeway*, London: Wildwood House, 1975

APULEIUS, *The Golden Ass* , trans. by Robert Graves, Harmondsworth: Penguin, 1950

ARAGON, Louis, Benjamin Péret, & Man Ray, *1929*, Paris: Allia, 2014

BARTHES, Roland, *A Lover's Discourse: Fragments*, trans. by Richard Howard, London: Jonathan Cape, 1979 [1977]

– *Camera Lucida*, trans. by Richard Howard, London: Jonathan Cape, 1982 [1980]

– *The Responsibility of Forms*, trans. by Richard Howard, New York: Hill and Wang, 1984 [1982]

– *Empire of Signs*, trans. by Richard Howard, London: Jonathan Cape, 1983 [1970]

– *Michelet*, translated by Richard Howard, New York: Hill and Wang, 1987 [1954]

BASHŌ, *The Narrow Road to the Deep North*, trans. by Noboyuki Yuasa, Harmondsworth: Penguin, 1966 [1694]

BAUDELAIRE, Charles, *Selected Poems*, trans. by Francis Scarfe, Harmondsworth: Penguin, 1973

BENJAMIN, Walter, *The Arcades Project*, trans. by Howard Eiland & Kevin McLaughlin, Cambridge, MA: Harvard University Press, 1999

BELLENGER, Sylvain, *Girodet*, Paris: Gallimard, 2005

BERGER, John, *Ways of Seeing*, London: British Broadcasting Corporation, 1972

BETTELHEIM, Bruno, *Freud and Man's Soul*, London: Chatto and Windus, 1983

BLAKE, William , *Visions of the Daughters of Albion*, London: Dent, 1932 [1793]
'The Ghost of Abel', in *William Blake, The Complete Illuminated Books*, London, Thames and Hudson, 2001 [1822], p. 479

BLACKWELL, Thoma, *An Enquiry into the Life and Writings of Homer*, London: Oswald, 1736

BLYTHE, R. H., *A History of Haiku*, Tokyo: Hokuseido Press, 1963

BORGES, Jorge Luis, *El Hacedor*, Madrid: Alianza, 1984 [1960]
– *A Personal Anthology*, ed. by Anthony Kerrigan, trans. by various, London: Jonathan Cape, 1968 [1961]
– *The Gold of the Tigers*, trans. by Alastair Reid, New York: E. P. Dutton, 1977 [1972]

BROWNE, Thomas, *Religio Medici, Urn Burial and Christian Morals*, Canterbury: Moreton, 1894

BRYANT, Barry, *The Wheel of Time Sand Mandala: Visual Scripture of Tibetan Buddhism*, New York: HarperCollins, 1992

BUBER, Martin, *I and Thou*, trans. by Ronald Gregor Smith, Edinburgh: T .& T. Clark, 1942 [1923]

BURKHARD, Balthasar, *Omnia*, Zurich: Scalo, 2005

BURNAGE, Sarah, Mark Hallett, & Laura Turner, *William Etty: Art and Controversy*, London: Philip Wilson, 2011

BURNS, Robert, *Songs from Robert Burns*, Collins: London and Glasgow, n.d., c. 1930

CALASSO, Roberto, *The Marriage of Cadmus and Harmony*, trans. by Tim Parks, London: Jonathan Cape, 1993 [1988]
– *Tiepolo Pink*, trans. by Alastair McEwen, London: Bodley Head, 2010 [2006]

CAMPBELL, Joseph, *The Hero with a Thousand Faces*, New York: Pantheon, 1949

CANNADINE, David, *Ornamentalism: How the British Saw Their Empire*, Oxford: Oxford University Press, 2002

CAPRA, Fritjof, *The Tao of Physics*, Boulder: Shambala, 1975

CESAROTTI, Melchior, *Poesie di Ossian*, Padova: Guiseppe Comino, 1772
– *Poesie di Ossian*, Nizza: Societa Tipografica, 1780

CHADWICK, Whitney, *Women, Art and Society*, London: Thames and Hudson, 1990

CHANG, Jolan, *The Tao of Love and Sex*, London: Wildwood House, 1977

CLARK, Kenneth, *The Nude*, Harmondsworth: Penguin, 1960

COHEN, Leonard, *Book of Longing*, London: Viking, 2006

COLLINGWOOD, R.G., *The Principles of Art*, Oxford: Clarendon, 1938

CONSTANTINE, Mildred, *Tina Modotti: A Fragile Life*, New York: Rizzoli, 1983

COOK, Albert S., *The Dream of the Rood*, Oxford: Clarendon, 1905

COOMARASWAMY, Ananda, *The Dance of Siva*, New York: Sunwise Turn, 1918

COZART, Daniel, *The Sand Mandala of Vajrabhairava*, Ithaca, NY: Snow Lion, 1995

DANTE (Dante Alighieri), *Inferno*, trans. by Thomas G. Bergin, New York: Appleton Century Crofts, nd: c. 1968 [1320]

DATER, Judy, *Imogen Cunningham: A Portrait*, Boston: New York Graphic Society, 1979

DAVIES, David, *El Greco: Mystery and Illumination*, National Galleries of Scotland, 1989

D'AVOINE, Pierre, 'Alexandria Library Competition', in Diamond, Rosamund & Wilfried Wang, *Reality and Project: Four British Architects: Armstrong Associates / Pierre d'Avoine / Tony Fretton / Tim Ronalds*, London: 9H Publications, 1990, pp. 29–31

DONNE, John, *Elegies and the Songs and Sonnets*, ed. by Helen Gardner, Oxford: Clarendon, 1965

DOUGLAS, Gavin, *The Poetical Works of Gavin Douglas Volume II*, edit. by John Small, Edinburgh: William Paterson, 1874

DUBOY, Philippe, *Jean Jacques Lequeu. An Architectural Enigma*, London: Thames and Hudson, 1986

DUNN, Richard, *Mannig-Faltig / Mani-fold*, Berlin: Jovis, 2005

DWELLY, Edward, *The Illustrated Gaelic-English Dictionary*, Glasgow: MacLaren, 1949

ECO, Umberto, *The Name of the Rose*, trans. by William Weaver, Harcourt Brace Jovanovich, 1983 [1980]

– *Postscript to the Name of the Rose*, trans. by William Weaver, New York: Harcourt Brace Jovanovich, 1984

– *Reflections on the Name of the Rose*, translated by William Weaver, London: Secker and Warburg, 1985

– *How to Write a Thesis*, trans. by Caterina Mongiat Farina & Geoff Farina, Cambridge: Massachusetts Institute of Technology, 2015 [1977]

EINSTEIN, Albert, *Ideas and Opinions*, New York: Bonanza, 1954

ELSEN, Albert E., *In Rodin's Studio: A photographic record of sculpture in the making*, Oxford: Phaidon, 1980

ENGELMAN, Edward, *Sigmund Freud: Berggasse 19, Vienna*, trans. by Lonnie R. Johnson, Vienna: Universe, 1998 [1993]

Euler, Walter, *Giotto Frescoes: The Scrovegni Chapel in Padua*, translated by Britta M. Charleston, Berne: Hallwag, 1969 [1968]

Evans, Tom, & Mary Anne Evans, *Shunga: The Art of Love in Japan*, London: Paddington Press, 1975

Fantelli, Pier Luigi, & Franca Pellegrini, *Il Palazzo della Ragione in Padova*, Verona: Cierre, 2000

Finlay, Ian Hamilton, *Nature over again after Poussin*, Glasgow: University of Strathclyde, 1980

Fitzgerald, Edward, *Rubaiyat of Omar Khayyam*, London: Zodiac Books, 1945 [1859]

Frazer, James, *The Golden Bough*, London: Macmillan, 1890

Freitag, Barbara, *Sheela-na-Gigs: Unravelling an Enigma*, London: Routledge, 2004

French, A. P. (ed.), *Einstein: A Centenary Volume*, Cambridge, MA: Harvard University Press, 1979

Freud, Sigmund, *Civilization and its Discontents*, trans. by Joan Riviere, London: Hogarth Press, 1939 [1929]

Freud Museum, *20 Maresfield Gardens: A Guide to the Freud Museum*, London: Serpent's Tail, 1998

Forman, Bedrich, *Borobudur: The Buddhist legend in stone*, trans. by V. J. Zizka, Leicester: Magna, 1992 [1980]

Foscari, Guilia, *Elements of Venice*, Zurich: Lars Muller, 2014

Gamwell, Lynn, & Richard Wells, *Sigmund Freud and Art: His Personal Collection of Antiquities*, Binghampton: State University of New York, 1989

Garfield, Leo & Edward Blishen, *The God Beneath the Sea*, ill. by Charles Keeping, London: Longman, 1970

Gaskill, Howard (ed.), *The Reception of Ossian in Europe*, London: Continuum, 2004

GEDDES, Patrick, *Cities in Evolution*, London: Williams and Norgate, 1915

GEOFFROY-SCHNEITER, Bérénice, *Gandhara: The Memory of Afghanistan*, trans. by David Wharry, New York: Assouline, 2001 [2000]

GILLANDERS, Robin, *Little Sparta: Portrait of a Garden*, Edinburgh: National Galleries of Scotland, 1998

GINSBERG, Allen, *Ankor Wat*, with photographs by Alexandra Lawrence, London: Fulcrum Press, 1968

GOETHE, Johann Wolfgang von, *The Sufferings of Young Werther*, trans. by Bayard Quincy Morgan, London: John Calder, 1957 [1774, 1787]

GOODWILLIE, Edward, *The World's Memorials of Robert Burns*, Detroit: Waverley Publishing, 1911

GUNN, Neil, 'Highland Space', *Saltire Review*, Vol. 6, No. 23, 45–48, 1961

GUTH, Alan .H, & Paul J. Steinhardt, 'The inflationary universe', *Scientific American*, Vol. 250, Issue 5, 116–28, 1984

HAFIZ, *The Rubaiyat of Hafiz*, trans. by Syed Abdul Majid & L. Cranmer-Byng, London: John Murray, 1910

HARADA, Jiro, *The Gardens of Japan*, London: The Studio, 1928

HARTLEY, L. P., *The Go-Between*, London: Hamish Hamilton, 1953

HEANEY, Seamus, *The Cure at Troy: A Version of Sophocles' Philoctetes*, New York: Farrar, Straus and Giroux, 1991

– *The Burial at Thebes: Sophocles' Antigone*, London: Faber, 2004

HEMANS, Felicia, *Poems*, Edinburgh: William Blackwood, 1865

HENDERSON, Hamish, *Collected Poems and Songs*, Edinburgh: Curly Snake Publishing, 2000

HERZOG, Lena, *Pilgrims: Becoming the Path Itself*, London: Arcperiplus, 2002

HESSE, Hermann, *My Belief: Essays on Life and Art*, trans. by Denver Lindley, New York: Farrar, Straus and Giroux, 1974

– *The Glass Bead Game*, trans. by R. Winston and C. Winston, Harmondsworth: Penguin, 1973 [1943]

HOKUSAI, Katsushika, *One Hundred Views of Mount Fuji*, London: Thames and Hudson, 1988 [1849]

HOLTON, Brian, *Staunin Ma Lane: Chinese Verse in Scots and English*, Bristol: Shearsman, 2016

HOMER, *Iliad*, trans. by James Macpherson, London: Becket and DeHondt, 1773

– *Odyssey*, trans. by E. V. Rieu, Harmondsworth: Penguin, 1945

– *Iliad*, trans. by E. V. Rieu, Harmondsworth: Penguin, 1950

HOOKS, Margaret, *Tina Modotti*: London: Phaidon, 2002

HOROVITZ, Michael (ed.), *Children of Albion: Poetry of the 'Underground' in Britain*, Harmondsworth: Penguin, 1969

HUGHES, Ted, *Tales from Ovid*, London: Faber, 1997

JAMES, William, 'The Psychology of Belief', *Mind* Vol. 14, No. 55, Jul., 1889, 321–352

JOHNSTON, Alan, *Tactile Geometry*, London: Bartha Contemporary, 2015

JOHNSON, James, & Robert Burns, *The Scots Musical Museum 1787–1803*, Aldershot: Scolar Press, 1991

JUDD, Donald, 'Some Aspects of Color in General and Red and Black in Particular', *Artforum* 32, No. 10. Summer 1994, 70–80, 110–113

KARPELES, Eric, *Paintings in Proust: A Visual Companion to 'In Search of Lost Time'*, London: Thames and Hudson, 2008

KEBLE, John, *The Christian Year*, London: Blackie, nd, c. 1903

KHANNA, Madhu, *Yantra: The Tantric Symbol of Cosmic Unity*, London: Thames & Hudson, 1979

KITCHEN, Paddy, *A Most Unsettling Person*, London: Gollancz, 1975

Kojève, Alexandre, *Introduction to the Reading of Hegel: Lectures on the Phenomenology of Spirit*, assembled by Raymond Queneau, ed. by Allan Bloom, trans. by James H. Nichols, Ithaca, NY: Cornell University Press, 1980

Lee, Ang, *Programme Notes: Crouching Tiger Hidden Dragon*, London: Curzon Cinema, 2001

Le Corbusier, *Towards a New Architecture*, trans. by Frederick Etchells, London: The Architectural Press, 1946 [1923]

Le Guin, Ursula, *The Left Hand of Darkness*, New York: Ace, 1969

Le Normand-Romain, Antoinette & Christina Buley-Uribe, *Auguste Rodin: Drawings and Watercolours*, London: Thames and Hudson, 2006

Levy, Michael, *Painting in XVIII Century Venice*, London: Phaidon, 1959

Lewis, C. S., *An Experiment in Criticism*, Cambridge: Cambridge University Press, 1961

Liebetrau, Preben, *Oriental Rugs in Colour*, trans. by Katherine John, New York: Macmillan, 1963

Light, Michael & Andrew Chaikin, *Full Moon*, London: Jonathan Cape, 1999

Logue, Christopher, *War Music: From Homer's Iliad*, London: Jonathan Cape, 1981

Lorenz, Richard, *Imogen Cunningham: On the Body*, Boston: Bullfinch, 1998

Lull (Llull), Ramon, *Book of the Lover and the Beloved*, trans. by Edgar Allison Peers, London: Society For Promoting Christian Knowledge, 1928 [1283]

Macadam, Alta, *Venice*, Taunton: Blue Guide, 2014

McCurry, Steve, *Sanctuary: The Temples of Angkor*, London: Phaidon, 2002

Macdonald, Donald, *Tales and Traditions of the Lews*, Stornoway: Macdonald, 1967

MacDonald, George, *George MacDonald: An Anthology*, ed. by C. S. Lewis, London: Geoffrey Bles, 1946

– *Lilith*, Grand Rapids: Eerdmans, 1981 [1895]

MacDonald, Malcolm, *Angkor*, with photographs by Loke Wan Tho, London: Jonathan Cape with Donald Moore Books, 1965

Macdonald, Murdo, 'A Basis for Library Design', *Edinburgh Architecture Research*, 12, 1985, 104–113

– (aka John Douglas), 'A Note from a Visiting Professor', in *Metronome: What is to be Done? Tokyo*, No. 11, ed.by Clémentine Deliss, Paris: Metronome Press, 2007, 142–143

– 'We all need shelter', in *Shelter: On Kindness*, ed. by Suzanne Davies, Melbourne: RMIT Gallery, 2009, 5–8

– 'Alan Johnston interviewed by Murdo Macdonald at HICA', in *Exhibitions 2014–2015*, Dalcrombie: Highland Institute for Contemporary Art, 2016, 36–45

Macfarlan, Robert, *The Poems of Ossian in the Original Gaelic with a Literal Translation into Latin by the late Robert Macfarlan – Together with a Dissertation on the Authenticity of the Poems by Sir John Sinclair, etc.*, London: Highland Society of London, 1807

Mac Ghill Eathain, Somhairle, *Dain do Eimhir agus Dain Eile*, Glasgow: MacLellan, 1943

MacGillivray, *The Last Wolf of Scotland*, Brighton: Pighog, 2013

MacLean, Sorley, *Reothairt is Contraigh / Spring tide and Neap tide*, Edinburgh: Canongate, 1977

MacLeod, Mary, *Gaelic Songs of Mary MacLeod*, trans. by James Carmichael Watson, Edinburgh: Oliver and Boyd, 1965

Macpherson, James, *Fragments of Ancient Poetry: Collected in the Highlands of Scotland*, second edition, Edinburgh: Hamilton and Balfour, 1760

– *Fingal, An Ancient Epic Poem In Six Books: Together with several other Poems, composed by Ossian the son of Fingal*, London: Becket and

De Hondt, 1762

– *Temora, An Ancient Epic Poem In Eight Books: Together with several other Poems, composed by Ossian, the Son of Fingal*, London: Becket and De Hondt, 1763

– *The Poems of Ossian*, Edinburgh: Oliver and Boyd, 1819

MADDOW, Ben, *Edward Weston: Seventy Photographs*, Boston: New York Graphic Society, 1978

MANDELSTAM, Osip, *Poems from Mandelstam*, trans. by R.H. Morrison, London and Toronto: Associated University Presses, 1990

MATTHEWS, John & Marian Green, *The Grail Seekers Companion*, illus. by Chesca Potter, London: Thorsons, 1986

MAYAKOVSKY, Vladimir, *Love is the Heart of Everything*, ed. by Bengt Jangfeld, trans. by Julian Graffy, Edinburgh: Polygon, 1986

MINFORD, John (translated), *I Ching (Yijing) The Book of Change*, New York: Viking, 2014

MISHIMA, Yukio, *Sun and Steel*, trans. by John Bester, London: Secker and Warburg, 1971

MOFFATT, James (translated), *The New Testament, a New Translation*, London: Hodder and Stoughton, 1933

MOOKERJEE, Ajit, & Madhu Khanna, *The Tantric Way*, London: Thames & Hudson, 1977

MUIRHEAD, L. Russell, *Venice*, Blue Guide, London: Benn, 1957

MURRAY, Graeme, *Poiesis: Aspects of Contemporary Poetic Activity*, Edinburgh: Fruitmarket Gallery, 1992

Musashi, Miyamoto, *A Book of Five Rings*, trans. by Victor Harris, London: Fontana, 1984

NASH, Paul, *Fertile Image*, ed. by Margaret Nash, London: Faber, 1951

NEEDHAM, Rodney, *Against the Tranquility of Axioms*, Berkeley, CA: University of California Press, 1983

NERUDA, Pablo, *Twenty Poems of Love and a Song of Despair*, trans. by W. S. Merwin, London: Cape, 1975

NEWALL, Christopher, *John Ruskin: Artist and Observer*, London: Paul Holberton, 2014

NITZE, William A., 'Spitzer's Grail Etymology', *The American Journal of Philology*, Vol. 66, No 3, 279–281, 1945

NOVALIS, 'Aphorisms', trans. by Michael Hamburger, in *New Road: Directions in European Art and Letters*, London: Grey Walls Press, 1945

OGBURN, Charlton, *The Marauders*, London: Hodder & Stoughton, 1960

OKAKURA, Kakuzo, *The Book of Tea*, Edinburgh: T. N. Foulis, 1919

OWEN, Wilfred, *The Collected Poems of Wilfred Owen*, ed. by C. Day Lewis, London: Chatto and Windus, 1982

PEELE, George, *The Love of King David and Fair Bethsabe*, Oxford: Malone Society, 1912 [1599]

PETRARCH (Francesco Petrarca), *Selections from the Canzoniere and other works*, trans. by Mark Musa, Oxford: Oxford University Press, 1985

PÉRET, Benjamin, Louis Aragon, and Man Ray, *1929*, Paris: Éditions Allia, 2014

PIGNATTI, Terisio, *Carpaccio*, trans. by James Emmons, Lausanne: Skira, 1958

PIRSIG, Robert M., *Zen and the Art of Motorcycle Maintenance: An Enquiry into Values*, London Bodley Head, 1974

PORTER, Eliot, *In Wildness is the Preservation of the World*, New York: Ballantyne, 1971

PRETTEJOHN, Elizabeth, *Beauty and Art*, Oxford: Oxford University Press, 2005

PROUST, Marcel *Against Sainte-Beuve and Other Essays*, trans. by John Sturrock, London: Penguin, 1994

PYLE, Andrew, *Key Philosophers in Conversation The Cogito Interviews*, London: Routledge, 1999

Raine, Kathleen, *Blake and Tradition*, Princeton: Princeton University Press, 1968

Rawson, Philip, *Tantra: The Indian Cult of Ecstasy*, London: Thames and Hudson, 1973

Read, Herbert, *The Meaning of Art*, London: Faber, 1931

Reiach and Hall Architects, *Stravaigers: In a Fading Light*, Edinburgh: Privately Printed, 2016

Rich, Adrienne, *The Fact of a Doorframe: Poems Selected and New 1950–1984*, New York: Norton, 1984

Rossetti, Christina, *Poems*, London: Blackie, nd, c. 1906

Rossetti, Dante Gabriel, *The New Life (La Vita Nuova) of Dante Alighieri*, London: Ellis & Elvey, 1903

Ruskin, John, *The Seven Lamps of Architecture*, London: Smith, Elder and Co., 1849

– *Modern Painters Volume 2*, third edition, London: Smith, Elder and Co., 1851

– *The Seven Lamps of Architecture*, London: Smith, Elder and Co., 1855

– 'Preface', *The Seven Lamps of Architecture*, Orpington: George Allen, 1880

– *Lectures on Landscape Delivered at Oxford in Lent Term 1871*, Orpington and London: George Allen, 1897

– *Ruskin on Pictures: Turner at the National Gallery and in Mr. Ruskin's Collection*, London: George Allen, 1902

– *Giotto and his Works in Padua*, London: George Allen, 1905

– *Unto this Last*, London: Dent, 1913

– *The Lamp of Beauty*, ed. by Joan Evans, London: Phaidon, 1959

Ryokan, *One Robe, One Bowl*, trans. by John Stevens, New York and Tokyo: Weatherhill, 1977

Sackville-West, Vita, & Harold Nicolson, *Another World Than This: An Anthology*, London: Michael Joseph, 1945

Schick, Jurgen, *The Gods are Leaving the Country*, trans. by Philip H. Pierce, Bangkok: Orchid Press, 1998 [1989]

Schmitt, Pierre, *The Isenheim Altar*, Berne: Hallwag, 1960

Schopenhauer, Arthur, *Essays and Aphorisms*, trans. by R. J. Hollingdale, Harmondsworth: Penguin, 1976

Scott, Walter, *Poetical Works*, vols. 1–4, 'Minstrelsy of the Scottish Border', Edinburgh: Cadell, 1833–4

– *Miscellaneous Prose Works*, vol. 25, Edinburgh: Cadell, 1836

Sesshū, *The Trip to Sesshū, The 500th anniversary of Sesshū's death*, Yamguchi: Yamaguchi Prefectural Museum of Art, 2006

Seton, Ernest Thompson, *Two Little Savages*, New York: Grosset and Dunlap, 1911

Shakespeare, William, *The Most Excellent and Lamentable Tragedy of Romeo and Juliet*, Harmondsworth: Penguin, 1937

– *The Tragedy of Macbeth*, Harmondsworth: Penguin, 1940

– *Hamlet*, Cambridge: Cambridge University Press, 1948

– *The Tragedy of Othello the Moor of Venice*, Harmondsworth: Penguin, 1955

– *The Tempest*, Harmondsworth: Penguin, 1955

Sleeman, Alison, 'Ha-ha Hegel', in *Chapman 78–79: Ian Hamilton Finlay*, Edinburgh: Chapman, 1994

Somerville, Mary, *Queen of Science: Personal Recollections of Mary Somerville*, ed. by Dorothy McMillan, Edinburgh: Canongate, 2001

Strachan, Gordon, *Chartres: Sacred Geometry, Sacred Space*, Edinburgh: Floris, 2003

Stevenson, Robert Louis, *Treasure Island*, Tusitala Edition, London: William Heinemann, 1924 [1883]

Stewart, D. C., *The Setts of the Scottish Tartans*, Edinburgh: Oliver and Boyd, 1950

Stokes, Adrian, *Venice: An Aspect of Art*, London: Faber, 1945

Sophocles, *The Theban Plays*, trans. by E. F. Watling, Harmondsworth: Penguin, 1947

– *King Oedipus: Illustrated by Kenneth J. McQueenie*, trans. by J. T. Sheppard & Richard Appignanesi, London: Abacus, 1986

Spies, Werner, *Focus on Art*, trans. by Luna Carne-Ross & John William Gabriel, New York: Rizzoli, 1982 [1979]

Spitzer, Leo, 'The Name of the Holy Grail', *The American Journal of Philology*, Vol. 65, No 4. 354–363, 1944

Staley, Allen, & Hilary Underwood, *Painting the Cosmos: Landscapes by G. F. Watts*, Compton: Watts Gallery, 2006

Sun Tzu, *The Art of War*, trans. by John Minford, London: Penguin, 2003

Tagore, Rabindranath, *Gitanjali: Song Offerings*, London: Macmillan, 1913

Tanizaki, Jun'ichirō, *In Praise of Shadows*, trans. by Thomas Harper & Edward Seidensticker, Sedgwick: Leete's Island Books, 1977

Tedlock, Barbara, & Dennis Tedlock, 'Text and Textile: Language and Technology in the Arts of the Quiché Maya', *Journal of Anthropological Research*, Vol. 41, No. 2, 121–146, 1985

Tennyson, Alfred, *Idylls of the King*, London: Henry S. King, 1874

– *The Death of Oenone, Akbar's Dream and Other Poems*, London: Macmillan, 1892

Thomson, George (ed.), *A Select Collection of Original Scottish Airs with Accompaniments by Haydn and Beethoven*, Edinburgh: Thomson, 1818

Turnbull, Gael, *A Trampoline*, London: Cape Goliard, 1968

–*Scantlings*, London: Cape Goliard, 1970

Vallance, Aymer, *Old Crosses and Lychgates*, London: Batsford, 1933

Virgil, *Doomed Love*, trans. by W. F. Jackson Knight, London: Penguin, 2007

Waddell, Helen, *Lyrics from the Chinese*, London: Constable, 1913

– *Mediaeval Latin Lyrics*, London: Constable, 1929

Waddington, C. H., *Behind Appearance*, Edinburgh: Edinburgh University Press, 1969

– *Tools for Thought*, London: Jonathan Cape, 1977

WAITE, Lorna J., *The Steel Garden*, Edinburgh: Word Power, 2011

WALKER, Barbara G., *The Woman's Dictionary of Symbols and Sacred Objects*, New York: Harper San Francisco, 1990

WATT, Judith, *Alexander McQueen, The Life and the Legacy*, London: SevenOaks, 2014

WATTS, Mary, *The Word in the Pattern, A Key To The Symbols On The Walls Of The Chapel At Compton*, London: Ward, nd, c. 1899

– *The Word in the Pattern, A Key To The Symbols On The Walls Of The Chapel At Compton*, second edition, enlarged, London: Astolat Press, 1904

WIESENDANGER, Mario, 'Bernstein's Principle of Equal Simplicity and Related Concepts', in Mark L. Latash (ed.), *Progress in Motor Control Volume One, Bernstein's Traditions in Movement Studies*, Champaign, IL: Human Kinetics, 1998

WILHELM, Richard, *The I Ching or Book of Changes*, translated by Cary F. Baynes, London: Routledge and Kegan Paul, 1951

WILKINSON, W. A. C., & N. H. Wilkinson, *The Dragon Book of Verse*, Oxford: Clarendon, 1935

WITTGENSTEIN, Ludwig, *Tractatus Logico-Philosophicus*, trans. by David Pears & Brian McGuinness, London: Routledge Kegan Paul, 1961 [1921]

– *Remarks on Frazer's Golden Bough*, ed. by Rush Rhees, trans. by A. C. Miles, Retford: Brynmill Press, 1979 [1967]

WRIGHT, Thomas, *The Life of William Blake*, Olney: Thomas Wright, 1929

YOUNG, Emily, *Siamo Tutti I Figli Della Pietra, We Are Stone's Children*, London: Fine Art Society, 2013

YOUNG, Wayland, *Eros Denied*, London: Weidenfeld and Nicolson, 1965

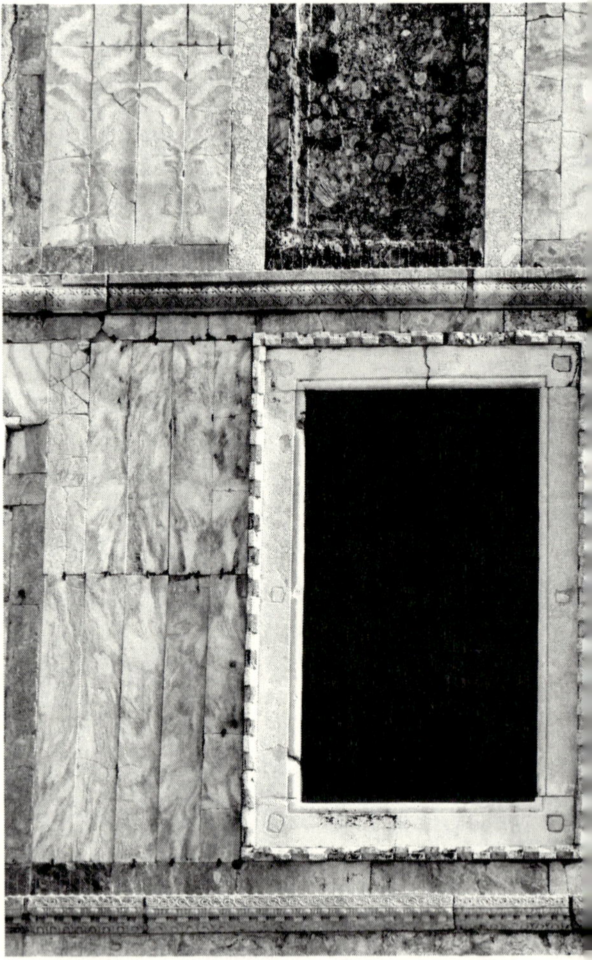

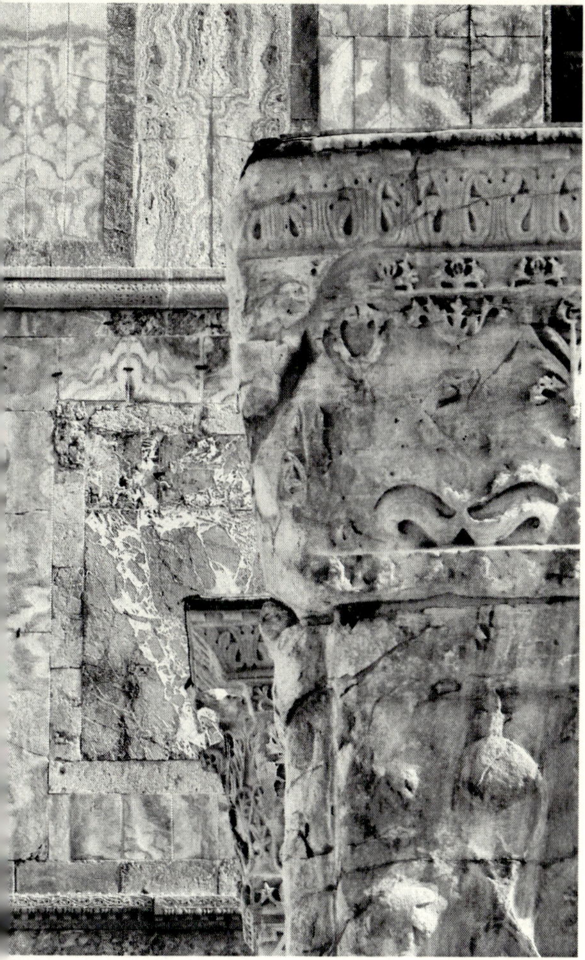